Working in the [

Working in the Dark focuses on the authors' understanding of an individual's pre-suicide state of mind, based on their work with many suicidal individuals, with special attention to those who attempted suicide while in treatment. The book explores how to listen to a suicidal individual's history, the nature of their primary relationships and their conscious and unconscious communications.

Campbell and Hale address the searing emotional impact on relatives, friends and those involved with a person who tries to kill themself, by offering advice on the management of a suicide attempt and how to follow up in the aftermath. Establishing key concepts such as suicide fantasy and pre-suicidal states in adolescents, the book illustrates the pre-suicide state of mind through clinical vignettes, case studies, reflections from those in recovery and discussions with professionals.

Working in the Dark will be of interest to social workers, probation officers, nurses, psychologists, counsellors, psychotherapists, psycho-analysts and doctors who work with those who have attempted suicide or are about to do so.

Donald Campbell is a qualified child, adolescent and adult psychoanalyst and a Training Analyst and Supervisor at the British Psychoanalytical Society. He has worked for thirty years as Principal Child and Adult Psychotherapist at the Portman Clinic. Campbell has lectured, taught widely and published papers and chapters on the subjects of suicide, violence, child sexual abuse, adolescence, shame and horror films.

Rob Hale trained originally in psychiatry and psychoanalysis and held a research post at St Mary's Hospital in London where, for five years, he worked closely with people who had attempted suicide. Hale has treated suicidal patients in long-term psychotherapy, and for thirty-five years worked at the Portman Clinic with those who act out in a violent or sexually deviant way.

'It's subject notwithstanding – what a brilliant, much-needed and ultimately hopeful-helpful book this is! The experience, if not the facts, of suicide remain taboo. The authors, based on nearly a century of combined clinical experience, expound its psychic meaning, developmental origins and therapeutic implications in ways relevant and accessible to all mental health practitioners. Robustly yet flexibly psychoanalytic, they demonstrate the paradox of suicide as 'an attempt to live at the cost of life itself', outline the '10 danger signals' of suicide for professionals, and illuminate the underlying phantasies inherent in the suicidal act. Heeded, this book will be a life-saver!'

Professor Jeremy Holmes, *MD, FRCPsych, University of Exeter, UK*

'The authors' unrivalled knowledge and experience garnered over many years is distilled to present a rich and compelling approach to suicide and therapeutic practice with suicidal people. The exploration of the influential concept of the pre-suicide state makes sense of suicidal motivations, explains the strong and often seemingly strange counter-transference responses encountered in this work and why working with suicidal people can draw negative reactions from professionals. Challenging conventional wisdom, *Working in the Dark* demonstrates that understanding unconscious suicide fantasies underpinning suicidal behaviour is essential to prevent the dangers of repeated suicide attempts.'

Professor Stephen Briggs, *University of East London, UK*

'Given the exceptional combination of clinical experience in dealing with suicide and self-harm, and the theoretical sophistication that Don Campbell and Rob Hale bring to the understanding of deeply disturbed people, I was prepared for a very significant contribution and I was not disappointed. The reason that you really do need to read this book from beginning to end is because of the help it brings to all of us who in our daily professional lives need to survive the trauma of working with people in the extremes of crises of mind and relationships. This is not just a book for the young, inexperienced staff who are usually, and often inappropriately, left to deal with the emotional complexities of those who have tried to harm themselves. No matter how long you have been in the field you will time and again find help, insight and support in this very valuable book.'

John, Lord Alderdice, *FRCPsych, University of Maryland, Baltimore, USA*

Working in the Dark

Understanding the pre-suicide state of mind

Donald Campbell and Rob Hale

Routledge
Taylor & Francis Group

LONDON AND NEW YORK

First published 2017
by Routledge
2 Park Square, Milton Park, Abingdon, Oxon OX14 4RN

and by Routledge
711 Third Avenue, New York, NY 10017

Routledge is an imprint of the Taylor & Francis Group, an informa business

British Library Cataloguing in Publication Data
A catalogue record for this book is available from the British Library.

Library of Congress Cataloging in Publication Data
Names: Campbell, Donald, author. | Hale, Rob (Robert), author.
Title: Working in the dark : understanding the pre-suicide state of mind /
Donald Campbell and Rob Hale.
Description: London ; New York : Routledge, 2017.
Identifiers: LCCN 2016012311| ISBN 9780415645423 (hardback) | ISBN
9780415645430 (pbk.) | ISBN 9781315731490 (ebook)
Subjects: LCSH: Suicidal behavior. | Suicide.
Classification: LCC RC569 .C36 2017 | DDC 616.85/8445--dc23
LC record available at https://lccn.loc.gov/2016012311

ISBN: 978-0-415-64542-3 (hbk)
ISBN: 978-0-415-64543-0 (pbk)
ISBN: 978-1-315-73149-0 (ebk)

Typeset in Times
by Saxon Graphics Ltd, Derby

MIX
Paper from
responsible sources
FSC
www.fsc.org   FSC® C013056

Printed and bound in Great Britain by
TJ International Ltd, Padstow, Cornwall

To Lizzie Campbell and Lizzie Hale

Contents

Acknowledgements   xiii

Introduction   1

1 Attitudes about suicide over the ages   7

2 Suicide and mental illness   11
Personality constellations in suicidal behaviour 14

3 Psychoanalytic understanding of suicide   18
Historically 18
Contemporary perspectives 21
Acting out 24
Suicide fantasies 26

4 The Core Complex   30
Ruthless and sadistic violence 31
The suicidal process 33
The pre-suicide state 35

**5 Suicide fantasies and the pre-suicide state of
mind**   43

6 How learning from the patient generates theory   51
Countertransference during a pre-suicide state 54

7   The role of the father in the pre-suicide state   57

8   Pre-suicide states in adolescence   63
The impact of puberty and adolescent development 63
The impact of puberty on the body image 65
The female body image 66
The male body image 67
Homosexuality in adolescence 68
Identification with the aggressor, asceticism, altruism
    and intellectualization 70
Masturbation in adolescence 71

9   Implications for the professional   74
Ten danger signals 75
Management of a suicide attempt 80
Assessment following a suicidal act 82
The aftermath of completed suicide 88
The impact of a suicide on the professional 89
Personal reactions to the death by suicide of one's
    patient 90
The response within the institution 93
The coroner's court 94

10   Self-mutilation   97

11   A patient's account   105

12   Conclusion   111

Index   113

Acknowledgements

We have always relied on the support and supervision of colleagues. It is humbling and sometimes embarrassing, but we are convinced that we could not have worked over many years with suicidal patients without the support and insight of colleagues who are too numerous to name. However, we would like to thank several colleagues who will represent those to whom we have brought our problems, doubts and anxieties over the years. In the early days we benefited from Egle Laufer's generous advice and long experience of work with suicidal adolescents. Many of our patients at the Portman Clinic were suicidal or became so when their defences broke down, and we are especially grateful to Mervin Glasser and our Portman colleagues to whom we brought these patients for their wisdom and help in holding the psychoanalytic frame. We would also like to thank Professor Robin Priest and Jan Tranter for their encouragement at St Mary's Hospital.

We have also been inspired by those who have written about suicide, again too numerous to name them all, but two papers have been especially influential: Freud's *Mourning and Melancholia* (1917 [1915]), which remains for us the seminal work in the understanding of the process of turning aggression against the self, and *Devices of Suicide* (1980) by Terry Maltsberger and Dan Buie, which was a welcome confirmation of our thinking by experienced psychoanalytic colleagues.

Finally, our wives, both named Lizzie, deserve a special mention in dispatches for their support and understanding during the inevitable times when we brought home our anxiety about a patient's life that seemed to be in the balance.

Introduction

Good creatures do you love your lives
And have you ears for sense?
Here is a knife like other knives
That cost me eighteen pence
I need but stick it in my heart
And down will come the sky
And earth's foundations will depart
And all you folk will die.

A. E. Housman (1939)

We have written this book for people who work with those who have threatened to stick a knife in their heart. It is intended for social workers, probation officers, nurses, psychologists, counsellors, psychotherapists, psychoanalysts and doctors who work with adolescents and adults who have attempted suicide or are about to do so. Our motivation for writing about pre-suicide states arises out of our own experiences with individuals who made suicide attempts while we were working with them. We felt that the only experience that is more painful and disturbing for a professional than their patient's attempted suicide is their patient's success in killing themselves. That is every practitioner's dread. For that reason, we tried to understand the patient's state of mind prior to making an attempt on their life. We found in understanding the pre-suicidal state of mind, we were able to intervene with our patients in ways that reduced the risk of self-murder. We hope that by passing what we have learned on to others they may find it helpful in keeping their suicidal patients alive.

This is how each of us came to write this book.

Rob Hale:

In the early 1970s, I was working as a psychiatrist-in-training at St Mary's Hospital in London. At that time the most common reason for being admitted to an acute general medical ward was an attempt at suicide, usually by overdose of drugs. It was more common, for example, than a coronary or a stroke or pneumonia. To give an idea of the size of the problem, in the year 1977 in the three hospitals making up the St Mary's group, there were 849 people admitted who had taken an overdose; this number does not include those who were admitted to surgical or orthopaedic wards who had tried to kill themselves by other means. It was customary at St Mary's, as at other hospitals, for the junior doctors to be sent to the medical wards to assess the seriousness of the attempt and to decide what treatment, if any, was appropriate.

Two factors immediately struck me at the time. First that, with the exception of drug addicts, these people were the most unpopular patients on the ward or in the casualty department. As an example of this, there was one ward sister who prided herself that she could provoke the patient to discharge themselves whilst they were still on the trolley and thereby avoid messing up one of her beds which were destined for 'proper patients'. Was it merely that they had brought their misfortune on themselves or were the staff responding to a deeper communication? Could it be that attempting suicide represented an attack on what the hospital stood for – the capacity to heal?

Second, the psychiatrist sent to deal with the problem was often the most junior of the team, yet suicide was the act most dreaded by the team as a whole (apart from homicide). It would be analogous to asking the junior house officer to carry out the heart transplant. One of the most important jobs in the hospital was being carried out by the least qualified member of staff. A superficial justification would be staff shortages or that junior staff needed the training experience. I saw it, however, as an institutional condemnation of the act itself. I observed that the staff acted as though the patient had forfeited the right to proper treatment, and treating them inadequately was revenge for 'abusing' the system. It was a primitive system of tit for tat with strong moral overtones rather than mutual respect or concern for the patient. The theme of talion emerges for the first time, to which we will return later.

As a result of these observations, I realised that suicide has a purpose and a meaning and is a form of communication. However, my view was not encompassed by the medical model that I had been taught, which saw the role of the psychiatrist as diagnosing or excluding (treatable) mental illness. Suicidality was a symptom of a disease, but any meaning was largely irrelevant. The medical approach seemed to me initially useful but actually limited and not very interesting. It suited some patients but many sought an explanation that related their feelings and actions to their circumstances, their relationships and their life experiences. If some form of psychotherapy seemed right for the patient, it did so for me, too. I embarked on my own psychoanalytic training and qualified after five years.

The consequence of taking myself seriously was that I wanted to take my patients and their suicidality seriously. Encouraged by the professor for whom I was working, I applied for research grants from pharmaceutical companies. The paradox in this situation was that an overdose of antidepressants was the most common means of attempting suicide. The trade-off was that I would carry out pharmacological studies on the effects of certain antidepressants on suicidal ideation and behaviour. This provided me with an opportunity to immerse myself in the subject. While I was assessing and treating many, many patients, they were teaching me about the nature of suicide. The generous research grants (provided initially by Boots Pharmaceuticals and then by Ciba-Geigy) allowed me to work on the project full time, to employ a secretary and to establish myself in a small office on the medical admissions ward of St Mary's Hospital, Paddington, London. Over the next five years I saw nearly all those people admitted following a suicide attempt and built up close working relationships with nursing, medical and social work staff. I learned an enormous amount from talking to the staff about their reactions to and understanding of the patients. It was, of course, the patients themselves who taught me most about suicide. For the most part this was an assessment procedure on the medical ward leading to admission to the psychiatric ward or the offer of outpatient treatment, which the patient might or might not take up. The purpose and details of this process we cover later in this book; suffice it to say, however, only a small proportion of those that I saw ended up in long-term psychotherapy, with myself or anyone else, for analysis. At any given time during this period I would have two or three people in long-term psychotherapy, and it was significant that both of those who were my psychoanalytic training cases came via a suicide attempt.

When we were about three years into the project, one of the ward sisters suggested that we set up a small side room on the admissions ward where patients could 'legitimately' stay for up to four days for solely psychiatric or psychotherapeutic reasons (i.e. there did not need to be a medical 'excuse' for them to stay in hospital). The plan was strongly supported by the social workers as well as the physicians and obviously the ward sister and nurses who had suggested it in the first place. It was then quite surprising that when the proposal reached the hospital management committee it was two of the senior psychiatrists who opposed it, and it was turned down. It may be, of course, that there were many good reasons for rejecting the proposal, including the possibility that I was not a popular or acceptable colleague, but I could not eliminate from my mind the thought that this was another enactment of the countertransference evoked by suicide.

During my psychoanalytic training, I had been in seminars with Mervin Glasser from the Portman Clinic and had been fascinated by his ideas about pathological uses of the body. I was also in supervision with Adam Limentani for my second training case; he had run the Portman before Mervin. I applied for and got a job at the Portman in 1980 where (apart from a short spell in the neighbouring Tavistock Clinic) I have remained. Whilst it is a National Health Service clinic for people who carry out sexually deviant or violent acts, there are two very significant features to these patients. First, they employ their bodies (and often the bodies of others) to enact and communicate their feelings. Second, a large proportion of them have attempted suicide in the past or are dominated by such impulses in the present. Of course, the majority of people who have self destructive ideas or impulses are not violent or sexually deviant.

Donald Campbell:

The first stirrings of my curiosity about suicide, or more specifically about the ingredients of the pre-suicide state, occurred during my adolescence in the Midwest of the United States. Getting a driver's licence in the US is often viewed as a rite of passage, especially for young men. In the state where I grew up you could get your driver's licence as early as your sixteenth birthday. I can remember the competition among my friends to get their driver's licences as close to their sixteenth birthday as possible. Passing your driver's test, and it was practically unheard of to fail, generated excitement, a sense of new independence and macho potency. Sadly, every high school student knew a teenager who was subsequently killed in a car crash. I never looked at the statistics, but I had the impression that the death toll from auto accidents was higher among late adolescents than older age groups. I thought there must be something about adolescent hormones. Whether I was driving or a passenger of a teenage driver, I enjoyed the sense of speed and risk, showing off and feeling bigger than we were. I would never have thought about it in these terms in those days, but in retrospect, I was thinking, however briefly, that for some teenagers, driving a car fed some wish to deny reality in the exercise of omnipotent power, which overrode a self-protective instinct.

Although I worked with adolescents therapeutically and trained as a child psychotherapist from 1969 to 1973 at the Hampstead Child-Therapy Course and Clinic in London (now the Anna Freud Centre), I did not systematically study suicidal behaviour in adolescents until I worked at the Brent Consultation Centre from 1976 to 1989. Suicide attempts featured in the adolescents that we treated in psychoanalysis and psychotherapy, discussed weekly, and were written about in *Developmental Breakdown and Psychoanalytic Treatment in Adolescence* (1989), edited by Moses and Egle Laufer. I was also influenced by an earlier paper, 'Attempted Suicide and Self-Mutilation in Adolescence: Some Observations from a Psychoanalytic Research Project' (1972), written by Maurice Friedman, Mervin Glasser, Egle Laufer, Moses Laufer and Myer Wohl, who were part of a research group at the Brent Consultation Centre. (These contributions will be discussed further in Chapters 7 and 8.)

Meanwhile, I had joined the Portman Clinic (part of the Tavistock and Portman NHS Foundation Trust in London) in 1973 as a child and adult psychotherapist and found that many of my adolescent and adult patients had made suicide attempts. My adult psychoanalytic training (1973–76) at the British Psychoanalytical Society built on my psychoanalytic studies at the Hampstead Child-Therapy Course and Clinic, particularly Freud's 'Mourning and Melancholia' (1917 [1915]), which was a formative influence on my thinking about suicide. However, it was the anxiety generated by working with suicidal patients that motivated me to study and write about this disturbing subject. When Rob Hale joined the Portman, he brought with him a wealth of clinical experience and research data from his work at St Mary's Hospital, which is discussed later in the book. Rob and I embarked on a dialogue about suicide that has continued for the rest of our professional lives. Each of us has presented and published papers on various aspects of suicidal behaviour and together we wrote 'Suicidal Acts' as a chapter for *Textbook of Psychotherapy in Psychiatric Practice* (1991), which was edited by Jeremy Holmes.

In this book we have pulled together our thinking and clinical experience from the past forty years. We offer the reader a particular psychoanalytic perspective, which we have found helpful in understanding the processes, meanings and impact of acts of suicide. Although our view is compared, contrasted and, where possible, integrated with other views of suicide, we hope every reader will carry on this work for him or herself.

References

Freud, S. (1917 [1915]). Mourning and melancholia. In J. Strachey (Ed. and Trans.), *The standard edition of the complete psychological works of Sigmund Freud (Vol. 14)*. London: Hogarth Press.

Friedman, M., Glasser, M., Laufer, E., Laufer, M. & Wohl, M. (1972). Attempted suicide and self-mutilation in adolescence: Some observations from a psychoanalytic research project. *The International Journal of Psychoanalysis, 53*(2), 179–183.

Holmes, J. (1991). *Textbook of psychotherapy in psychiatric practice*. Churchill Livingstone.

Housman, A. E. (1939). *The collected poems of A. E. Housman*. London: Penguin Books.

Laufer, M. & Laufer, M. E. (1989). *Developmental breakdown and psychoanalytic treatment in adolescence: Clinical studies*. New Haven, CT US: Yale University Press.

Chapter 1

Attitudes about suicide over the ages

A glimpse of the history of suicide reveals the changing attitudes and conceptual frameworks. Suicide is as old as history and ubiquitous. Throughout the ages it has been variously regarded as an altruistic act, a crime against the state, a sin against religion and an immoral act. As Robin Anderson (2000), a psychoanalytic colleague, points out:

> In Europe during most of the Christian era, suicide was regarded with even greater condemnation, and therefore presumably fear, than murder. The unsuccessful suicide was not only punished severely, but the successful suicides could not be buried in an ordinary cemetery. They had to be buried at a crossroads either with a stake through the heart or with stones on top of the body to prevent their spirit rising and haunting the living.

Shakespeare (1914) refers to this in *A Midsummer Night's Dream* (Act Three, Scene II, 380–7) where Puck says:

> *And yonder shines Aurora's harbinger,*
> *At whose approach ghosts, wand'ring here and there,*
> *Troop home to churchyards. Damned spirit all,*
> *That in crossways and floods have burial,*
> *Already to their wormy beds are gone,*
> *For fear lest day should look their shame upon;*
> *They wilfully themselves exil'd from light,*
> *And must for aye consort with black-brow'd night.*

Here Shakespeare refers to the burial of murderers and suicides at crossroads and the 'floods' in which people had drowned themselves and are left permanently excluded from society even after their deaths.

The fear seemed to be that such a terrible act would come back and infect the living. (We will return to this early recognition of the impact of the suicide on others.)

Although we have now done away with these barbaric and superstitious practices, suicide was illegal in the United Kingdom until 1961, and it was still possible to be sent to prison for attempted suicide. Perhaps the law, without realising it, for a long time understood the unconscious intention of suicide. It is noteworthy that attempted suicide is still an offence in Singapore and people may still be sent to jail.

Until the end of the eighteenth century, suicide was seen as a crime against God. In the early nineteenth century this gave way to a model of disease in which suicide was seen either as a disease in itself – a special form of insanity or as a manifestation of a more general mental disorder not to be found in sane persons (Bourdin and Esquirol as cited in Berrios & Porter, 1995). Later, Durkheim (1951) introduced the first sociological perspective in his monumental work *Le Suicide*, which viewed suicide as a collective phenomenon, influenced by specific factors characterising the society in which it appeared – where social solidarity was strong, there would be little suicide, where it was weak, there would be more.

Modern medicine and psychiatry have studied the epidemiology, genetics and biology of suicide together with the influence of life events both personal and societal; also the impact of various forms of treatment – pharmacological, physical and psychological – on suicidal ideation and behaviour. Each is important but outside the scope of this book. There are excellent and compendious books, often multi-authored (e.g. Hawton & van Heeringen, 2000), which cover those various views of suicide. We restrict our task to a psychoanalytic study of suicide, and recommend *Essential Papers on Suicide* (1996) by Maltsberger and Goldblatt for those who are interested in the psychoanalytic papers that have influenced our thinking.

As a consequence of their study and treatment of suicidal individuals, psychoanalysts are in a position to extend and also to challenge various assumptions and part-truths that other professionals and laymen have made about suicide. As we hope will become clearer in this book, the psychoanalytic process gives us the opportunity to study in minute detail the many component parts of the self-destructive process, and its waxing and waning control over a person's life. Psychoanalytic theory has as its cornerstone the concept of the unconscious, which differentiates it from all other theories. It is in the unconscious that the fundamental suicidal fantasies reside; it is the purpose of analysis to make those fantasies conscious and thus more within the person's control. Obviously psychoanalytic treatment is time consuming and not available to many people, but the insights psychoanalysis provides can be extended and integrated into the management and treatment of any suicidal individual. It is our hope that this book will convince you, the reader, of the usefulness of the psychoanalytic model, both in general mental health settings and in specialist psychotherapy services.

Suicide is commonly held to be part of a depressive state in which the person feels that life is not worth living and that death is preferable. Certainly, sadness and pessimism are often present, but they do not in themselves account for the major drive towards suicide. A second assumption is that suicide is a cry for help. This is a view that may be influenced as much by the professional's need to help as it is by the patient's crying out for it. A third assumption is that suicide is a means of manipulating others. Again, this is in part true. A fourth assumption is that suicide can be a solitary or solipsistic act in which the person rationally decides to take leave of life. This has also been referred to as the rational suicide, or the suicide of anomie. Although such acts may occur, they are, in our experience, extremely rare. Each of these assumptions is only partly true, and, if taken as the whole truth, is misleading because they fail to recognise the complexity of the act and the centrality of the violence inherent in the suicidal act.

If a self-destructive act is examined superficially, the patient's conscious intentions may well confirm one of the popular assumptions about suicide. However, closer scrutiny of unconscious processes reveals the less acceptable face of suicide as an act aimed at destroying the self's body and tormenting the mind of another. The contradiction between a benign view of suicide and the perception of the act as violent or cruel may be apparent to the observer but is unlikely to be acknowledged by the patient. Usually, aggressive wishes are so unacceptable to the patient that they are relegated to the unconscious by repression. The patient, therefore, continues to deal with the contradiction between his conscious view of the suicide attempt and unconscious wishes by resisting any attempt to bring anger, sadism or aggressive intentions into consciousness.

Ambivalence and contradiction are at the centre of the suicidal act. A patient reported that he had taken 199 aspirins. One had fallen on the floor and he refused to take it because it might have germs on it. It would be potentially dangerous for a clinician to respond only to the patient's conscious wish to live, that is, to protect himself from germs, and not to pursue the intent behind swallowing the other 199 pills.

In the authors' opinion, therefore, to identify any self-destructive act as either suicide or parasuicide is both simplistic and incorrect. The most useful term is a suicidal act with the outcome unstated. Our working definition of the suicidal act is the conscious or unconscious intention at the time of the act to kill the self's body. We are proposing the concept of a split between the self and the body regarded as a separate object. Later, we will contrast this with acts of self-mutilation in which the intention is not to kill but to torture the body.

Although we have not studied the cross-cultural aspects of suicide in any detail, it is our experience that the fundamental dynamics are *remarkably* constant, although the precipitants and methods will be influenced by cultural and social phenomena. Much of the literature in other books and journals is devoted to this topic, so we will not dwell on it here.

Our purpose, then, is to provide a psychoanalytic view of the purposes, courses and impacts of suicidal acts. Our source material is our clinical experience to which we have sought to give our own theoretical structure, and our goal is to integrate this theory into that of other psychoanalysts. We start, however, by comparing the psychoanalytic view with that of mainstream psychiatry.

References

Anderson, R. (2000). Assessing the risk of self-harm in adolescents: A psychoanalytic perspective. *Psychoanalytic Psychotherapy, 14*(1), 9–21.

Berrios, G. E. & Porter, R. (1995). *A history of clinical psychiatry: The origin and history of psychiatric disorders*. New York, NY US: New York University Press.

Durkheim, E. (1951). *Le Suicide*. New York, NY US: Free Press.

Hawton, K. & van Heeringen, K. (2000). *The international handbook of suicide and attempted suicide*. New York, NY US: John Wiley & Sons Ltd.

Maltsberger, J. T. & Goldblatt, M. J. (1996). *Essential papers on suicide*. New York, NY US: New York University Press.

Shakespeare, W. (1914). *A midsummer night's dream*. London: Oxford University Press.

Chapter 2

Suicide and mental illness

In this chapter we want to look at some of the statistics of suicidal behaviour as well as some of the many descriptive profiles of the lives of those who attempt or succeed in suicide.

According to the World Health Organisation (2014), suicide is the eleventh most common form of death worldwide, accounting for about one million deaths per year. Add to this the fact that suicide rates in both US and UK are continuing to rise (particularly in middle-aged men) and the importance of the study of such acts is obvious; all this despite the development of extended suicide prevention programmes. Whether the statistics would have been even worse without these programmes is impossible to say. A recent commentary by Kamerow (2012), written from what would appear to be a very medical perspective, highlights these statistics and concentrates on risk factors and prevention strategies – both very important. What is missing, however, is any concept of an understanding of the suicidal act.

Although many psychiatric texts pay scant attention to the dynamics of suicide, a psychoanalytic book such as this should not diminish, by turn, the importance and usefulness of conventional, psychiatric and descriptive approaches. Unfortunately, professional identities often determine an all too narrow lens through which a suicidal act is viewed – to the detriment of the patient. The organic psychiatrist sees it in medical terms as the result of or as a by-product of an illness, a disturbance of brain biochemistry. The treatment is drugs which correct the imbalance. The sociologist sees it as the result of social pressures relating to economics, culture, religion, ethnicity, social deprivation and disadvantage. The remedy lies in altering, where possible, the social circumstances and pressures that a person is encountering on an individual basis or the disadvantage experienced by a group of people – for example, the loneliness of old age or financial adversity. The cognitive psychologist sees suicide as the result of the individual distorting or misperceiving interpersonal experiences, always giving them a negative connotation. The treatment is cognitive behavioural therapy or dialectical behavioural therapy. As for the psychotherapist or psychoanalyst, it is the dynamic approach set out in this book which we would espouse. Overall we would encourage a multidimensional approach, which attempts to integrate biological, social and psychological theories, since, if they represent part of the truth, they must ultimately be reconcilable. This is a tall order since each of us has chosen a profession or professional identity which makes sense of the world for us and to which we fall back often to the exclusion of other theoretical frameworks.

Let's look at the contribution of descriptive (organic) psychiatry, which aims to establish the presence or absence of defined mental illnesses on the basis of symptoms experienced by the patient or signs indicated to the observer by their behaviour. The way that these phenomena fluctuate throughout a person's lifetime is an important part of this assessment. Psychological autopsy, the process of making a retrospective diagnosis by examining all the known facts from whatever sources, has been widely used to establish diagnostic categories for those who kill themselves. The range of figures for individual suicide is high – with the incidence of depressive disorders varying between 37 percent and 90 percent. One wonders whether the diagnosis of depression is in the eye of the beholder. As Braithwaite (2012) observes, in response to Kamerow's article mentioned above:

> As depressive disorder is hugely over diagnosed in life (Aragonès, Piñol & Labad, 2006) what is there to suggest the same is not true in death? Recent prescription of antidepressants to a deceased subject or retrospective reports of insomnia, lethargy and low mood from family members do not automatically equate to a true diagnosis of depressive disorder. Yet the pragmatic methodology of psychological autopsy studies dictates precisely that (p. E8201).

There can be no doubt that mental illness plays an important role, but it is significant that the UK Government Confidential Inquiry (Appleby, Shaw & Amos, 1997) reveals that over 60 percent of people who kill themselves have not had any contact with psychiatric services. A review of American figures by Luoma and colleagues (Luoma, Martin & Pearson, 2002) reveals that of those people who kill themselves, only 33 percent had been in contact with secondary psychiatric services in the previous year, but 75 percent had been in contact with their GP. In the month prior to death, 20 percent had been in contact with mental health services whereas 50 percent had consulted their GP. It is impossible to say whether this indicates that the majority of those killing themselves are not mentally ill, or do not recognise it or wish to recognise it or, alternatively, do not see any purpose in consulting psychiatric services. However, as far as detection and prevention are concerned, the figures would suggest that we might be looking in the wrong place, since most psychiatric research concentrates on those in contact with secondary psychiatric services and ignores the vast majority who are not. Perhaps it is a reflection of the suicidal individual's ambivalence, the wish to communicate their distress and simultaneously their wish not to have it taken seriously, or to present it in a disguised form thus leaving their options open. The consequence if they do attempt or succeed in suicide is that the GP is left feeling both tricked and negligent. Perhaps, then, suicide prevention strategies should focus education and support on general practitioners and counsellors in general practice settings.

It may be more useful to consider Lonnquist's findings regarding the lifetime risks of death by suicide in individuals with specific psychiatric diagnoses (in Gelder, Andreasen, Lopez-Ibor & Geddes, 2000, p. 1038):

Thus, for example, people with an established diagnosis of manic-depression or major depressive illness have a one in ten to one in six chance of dying by suicide at some point in their lives (ibid.). The diagnosis of personality disorder is perhaps even more variable. However, a diagnosis of borderline personality disorder or psychopathic disorder also represents a considerable increase in the likelihood of suicidal acting out (Lonnquist, in Gedler et al., 2000).

Assessment is a role frequently carried out by a medically trained person and will include enquiring into the presence of symptoms of anxiety, both psychological and physical, as well as depression with the associated symptoms of, amongst others, sleep and appetite disturbance as well as low mood and pessimism. Suicide can occur whilst the individual is in a manic state, so excitability, argumentativeness and overactivity are important signs to be recognised. So, too, are the signs

Table 2.1 Psychiatric Diagnosis Lifetime Expectancy of Death by Suicide

1. Manic-depression/major depression	10–16%
2. Schizophrenia	4–13%
3. Alcoholism	7%
4. Drug dependency	13–18%

of a schizophrenic (psychotic) illness with the distortions of perception and hallucinatory experiences. Suffice it to say that if the therapist is at all worried that there may be, or may have been, evidence of 'organic' mental illness, it is important to seek a psychiatric assessment, since the pharmacological treatment of the illness may reduce the risk of suicide. It also establishes a professional contact which may prove useful if a subsequent admission to in-patient care becomes necessary. A medical and a psychoanalytic approach are far from mutually exclusive.

It is, therefore, crucial in assessing a suicidal individual to ask the relevant questions to identify the extent to which mental illness is currently present or has existed in the past, as there is evidence that the pharmacological treatment of the illness reduces the risk of suicide.

Personality constellations in suicidal behaviour

A paper by Apter (2004) confirms our view of the limitations of sole reliance upon assessment of psychiatric disorder in determining suicidal risks. Apter cites the frequent association between suicidal states and mental disorder, commenting, "These diagnostic indicators have low specificity, do not aid greatly the prediction of suicidal behaviour within diagnostic categories such as depression and do not shed light on the aetiology of suicidal behaviour" (p. 24). Apter hypothesises that there are three sets of personality constellations that may underlie a propensity towards suicidal behaviour:

1   *Narcissism, perfectionism and the inability to tolerate failure and imperfection, combined with an underlying schizoid personality structure that does not allow the individual to ask for help and denies him the comforts of intimacy.* In most cases these seem to be lifelong personality patterns not related to stress or periods of depression. Apter describes these people as using achievement as a kind of pseudo-mastery substitute for a lack of real interpersonal closeness, and they are especially vulnerable to catastrophic decompensation – a collapse of psychological functioning – in the form of a suicidal act. Shame and humiliation are triggers for suicidal acts in this group of people.

2   *Impulsive and aggressive characteristics combined with an over sensitivity to minor life events.* This sensitivity often leads to angry and anxious reactions with secondary depression. These people tend to use defences such as regression (the return to a more

childlike way of functioning), splitting (dividing the world into good and bad, black and white with no grey areas), dissociation (distancing oneself from the emotional meaning and impact of an event) and displacement (attributing the cause of a problem to someone else rather than the true author). They have frequently suffered childhood physical and/or sexual abuse, and there is often a history of alcohol or substance abuse in adult life. Apter links these characteristics to an underlying disturbance of serotonin metabolism (a biochemical substance responsible for transmission of nervous impulses in certain parts of the central nervous system), which he suggests is genetic in origin. However, given the high incidence of childhood traumatic events in this group of patients, and with the increasing knowledge of the biological consequences of child abuse, it seems possible that the biochemical abnormalities are at least to an extent determined or exacerbated by childhood trauma.

In adult life, these people are seen as impulsive, at times aggressive, with a low tolerance of frustration. They are often categorised as having a borderline personality disorder.

3 *Those persons whose suicidal behaviour is driven by hopelessness often related to an underlying depressive state.* Apter suggests that this hopelessness results from mental illness, such as affective disorder, schizophrenia or anxiety disorder, using the paradigm of underlying mental illness to account for the suicidal behaviour. Clearly this is the case when one encounters an individual who has a longstanding bipolar disorder (recurrent manic depression or recurrent depression), or a recurring schizophrenic illness. However, in our experience, in the majority of cases, the depressive state is a reaction to life circumstances and represents unconscious anger turned against the self.

Apter comments, 'Since the majority of patients with a psychiatric disorder do not commit or even attempt suicide it appears that a psychiatric disorder may be a necessary but not a sufficient risk factor for suicide. Therefore, one of the most pressing clinical research questions is to determine what factors above and beyond psychiatric disorder predispose to suicide' (p. 24).

An article by O'Connell, Chin, Cunningham & Lawlor (2004) highlights the increased risk of suicide in the elderly, a group of patients whom we increasingly encounter in clinical practice as psychotherapists, both because we now live longer but also because psychotherapists have come to regard therapy for the elderly as relevant and useful. These authors' central postulate is that ageing reduces the strength of our supportive social structures and exaggerates previous psychological and physical vulnerabilities. The consequences of suicide in the elderly can be as devastating to those close to them as is the death by suicide of a young person.

Suicide following childbirth presents a unique and perplexing situation. Normally suicide by violent means represents less than 20 percent of deaths. By contrast, in post-partum suicide over 80 percent of women killing themselves do so by violent means (Department of Health, 1998). As to why this is so atypical is unknown. The hormonal changes following childbirth may well be a causal factor in the very high incidence of depression in post-partum women with a predisposition to bipolar or unipolar affective disorder, but it is hard to see how this could account for the very different methods used.

The studies we have cited have been epidemiological and give crucial pointers to those most at risk. They are essentially nomothetic in that they seek to place the individual in a previously defined category. By contrast, the psychoanalytic approach is ideographic, seeking to establish the specific meaning of any person's actions by concentrating on an individual's uniqueness and their unique relationships within the common denominators of individuals who are vulnerable to suicide. We would suggest that, alongside other approaches, a psychoanalytic formulation contributes considerably to the management of suicidal states and can inform the contributions to care which may come, not only from psychiatrists and psychotherapists, but also general practitioners, psychiatric nurses, social workers and other professionals. Part of the skill of a diagnostic assessment is to explore which conceptual framework seems most relevant to the patient themselves in understanding their suicidal actions. It is usually futile to try to persuade a patient or their relatives that their actions were the result of dynamic interpersonal or unconscious motives when they believe, or want to believe, that it was caused by, say, abnormal biochemistry. It is a matter of what the patient can bear to hear.

There is often no single correct professional response to a suicidal act. For example, medication may well be indicated but it is important to recognise that merely to prescribe will not be sufficient, as this can easily be perceived by the patient as a rejection – that their feelings and fantasies do not have meaning, that the professional cannot cope with them or has insufficient concern to care for the patient in other ways. It is also important for teams of professionals to establish a common philosophy or way of understanding suicidal acts in order to minimise the patient's potential for splitting one member against another.

References

Appleby, L., Shaw, J. & Amos, T. (1997). National confidential inquiry into suicide and homicide by people with mental illness. *British Journal of Psychiatry 170*, 101–102.

Apter, A. (2004). Personality constellations in suicidal behaviour. *Imago-Napoli Then Padova, 11*(1), 5–28.

Aragonès, E., Piñol, J. L. & Labad, A. (2006). The overdiagnosis of depression in non-depressed patients in primary care. *Family Practice, 23*(3), 363–368. doi: 10.1093/fampra/cmi120

Braithwaite, R. (2012). Letter in response to 'Can suicide be prevented'. *British Medical Journal, 345,*8201. doi: http://dx.doi.org/10.1136/bmj.e8201

Department of Health. (1998). Why mothers die: Report on confidential enquiries into maternal deaths in the United Kingdom. London: RCOG Press.

Gelder, M., Andreasen, N., Lopez-Ibor, J. & Geddes, J. (2000). *New Oxford textbook of psychiatry*. Oxford: Open University Press.

Kamerow, D. (2012). Can suicide be prevented? *British Medical Journal, 345,* 7557. Doi: http://dx.doi.org/10.1136/bmj.e7557

Luoma, J. B., Martin, C. E. & Pearson, J. L. (2002). Contact with mental health and primary care providers before suicide: A review of the evidence. *The American Journal of Psychiatry, 159*(6), 909–916. doi: 10.1176/appi.ajp.159.6.909

O'Connell, H., Chin, A., Cunningham, C. & Lawlor, B. A. (2004). Recent developments: Suicide in older people. *British Medical Journal. 329,* 895–899.

World Health Organisation. (n.d.) Retrieved June 18, 2014, from www.who.int/topics/suicide/en/

Chapter 3

Psychoanalytic understanding of suicide

Historically

Suicide has for a long time been a focus of interest for psychoanalysts. In 1910, the Vienna Psychoanalytic Society organised a symposium entitled *On Suicide: With Particular Reference to Suicide Among Young Students* (Stekel, 1910). Contributors included Sigmund Freud, Alfred Adler and Wilhelm Stekel. It represented a turning point in the study of suicide, which had previously concentrated on external factors, for example, Durkheim's previously mentioned monumental works relating the incidence of suicide to social and geographical factors. Attention was now directed to the inner fantasy world of the individual, where the destructive and vengeful nature of suicide was recognised.

In Stekel's paper to the conference, he stated, 'I am inclined to feel that the principle of Talion plays the decisive role here. No one kills himself who has never wanted to kill another or at least wished the death of another' (p. 87). This paper laid the foundation for all subsequent psychoanalytic thinking on suicide.

Aggression turned against the self in suicide was taken up by Freud in his paper, 'Mourning and Melancholia' (1917 [1915]). Freud observed that in melancholia after a loss or a 'real slight or disappointment' coming from a person for whom there are strong ambivalent feelings, the hate originally felt towards the person may be redirected towards the self. He writes:

> It is this sadism alone that solves the riddle of the tendency to suicide, which makes melancholia so interesting – and so dangerous.

The analysis of melancholia now shows that the ego can kill itself only if ... it can treat itself as an object – if it is able to direct against itself the hostility which relates to an object and which represents the ego's original reaction to objects in the external world.

(Freud, 1917, p. 252)

The reader may wonder what Freud means by 'ego'. Identifying the complexity of the nature and function of the ego, as psychoanalysts understand it, is beyond the scope of this book. However, for our purposes, we want to highlight three characteristics of the ego: 1) it is a particular part of the mind, an agency, as it were, that is oriented to and responsible for compromise between the demands of reality, the instincts and the superego, 2) Freud's (1923) view that the ego is 'first and foremost a bodily ego' (p. 26) highlights the intimate reciprocity between the person's ego and his or her body, which is particularly relevant to our understanding the pre-suicide state, 3) the ego is constituted by identifications with important people in the person's life. The above quote from Freud is interesting because it implies both aspects of the concept of ego: an executive function that decides to kill, and refers to a self, which is the object of the murderous attack. We understand the use of the term 'object' in the same quote as a reference to an 'other' in this context, a part of the self that is experienced as 'not self'.

Although Freud did not write a paper specifically about suicide, references to motivation for suicide appear in his papers. Our overview of Freud's thinking about suicide is based on Litman's (1970; 1996) valuable paper, which collects Freud's thoughts about suicide from his papers and correspondence. Freud's clinical experience was the initial resource for his insights into suicide. Several of his patients were suicidal and one patient succeeded in killing himself (Freud 1901; Litman 1970, 1996, p. 203). He noted that suicide could represent self-punishment for guilt over rivalry and wishes for another's death, especially a parent (Freud, 1909, pp. 153–318; Freud, 1913, p. 154). He also knew about the role that identification with a suicidal parent, refusal to accept loss of sexual gratification, escape from humiliation and a cry for help play in suicidal behaviour. In addition, Freud understood the devastating impact that suicide can have on others and wish for revenge that motivates some suicides.

Psychoanalysts understand identification with one's parents to be a normal part of development, that is, an unconscious process by which aspects of our parents are taken in and become a largely unconscious part of how we behave and think of ourselves. This process begins as an effort to overcome the inevitable loss that the child experiences as it separates from its parents. Unconsciously the child thinks, 'If I cannot have mummy or daddy, I can be like them, and, in that way, be close to them'. When we refer to an unconscious phenomenon, as we have just now, we are simply referring to a thought or feeling of which we are not aware. We think of libido as sexual energy that is mobilised to preserve the self from threats to physical and psychological survival and underpinned by the instinct to preserve the species. This sexual energy generates pleasure when it is attached to the self (as in narcissism), another person (as in 'falling in love') or another inanimate object (such as a fetish).

Litman emphasises Freud's view that every suicide is multi-determined and his observation that self-destruction is present to some degree in very many more human beings than those that carry out a suicide fantasy. He quotes Freud:

> Even a conscious intention of committing suicide chooses its times, means and opportunity; and it is quite in keeping with this that an unconscious intention should wait for a precipitating occasion, which can take over a part of the causation and by engaging the subject's defensive forces, can liberate the intention from their pressure.
>
> (Freud, 1901, pp. 178–185)

We think it is worth identifying what we mean when we think of 'defensive forces' or defences, because these terms, like the term unconscious and libido, feature in our understanding of the pre-suicide state of mind. All defences operate unconsciously, have their roots in childhood, and aim to reduce anxiety by distorting thinking and memory, and creating symptoms. In this book, when we identify defences in patients we will try to indicate the anxieties and fears that motivate those defences and the protection that the defences afford the individual.

After 1920, Freud's clinical impressions, influenced by repetition compulsion and traumatic neurosis, were supported by biological and philosophical arguments to justify the existence of a death instinct. In melancholia, the punitive superego that drives the ego to death was understood as an expression of a death instinct, which some analysts think of as a universal instinctual drive towards self-destruction.

In melancholia, the ego gives itself up because it feels itself hated and persecuted by the superego instead of loved. Psychoanalysts differ in their views about the origins of the superego, but it is widely seen as a mental structure that contains parental injunctions and prohibitions, which the ego tries to live up to or abide by. When the ego is successful, it enjoys the superego's approval and protection. When the ego fails to live up to the superego's prescriptions or transgresses the superego's proscriptions, it experiences shame and guilt. We have often found that death by suicide symbolises or re-enacts a sort of abandonment of the ego by the superego. It is a situation similar to severe rejection by a loving and protecting mother (Freud, 1923, pp. 53–58).

In the suicidal individuals we have studied it is the body that is treated as, what in psychoanalytic terms would be regarded as a separate object (as though it were a separate person), and concretely identified with the lost loved and hated person, that is, a person for whom there are strong ambivalent feelings. Our understanding of suicidal patients is influenced by Freud's observations and begins with the view that in these patients a split in the ego has resulted in a critical and punitive superego perceiving the body and its impulses as a separate, bad or dangerous object. It is as though the ego carries out the punishment at the behest of the superego or offers the body as a sacrifice to a persecuting and vengeful superego.

Contemporary perspectives

Although some psychoanalytic writers, for example Bell (2001), refer to a death instinct to explain masochism and the turning of aggression against the self, we do not. Instead, like Litman, our clinical experience has led us to explain suicidal individuals by reference to: 1) splitting of the ego, whereby the ego takes its self as a good object and its body is experienced as a bad object that threatens the survival of the self and must be got rid of, 2) identificatory processes, in which aspects of others are taken in and become a part of the self, and 3) psychotic mechanisms, which have in common a withdrawal of a part of the self from reality.

Adams (1985) uses attachment theory and sociological research to argue that suicidal behaviour represents an attempt to repair early failures in primary attachments, which impair the suicidal individual's efforts to form stable and non-pathological relationships in adolescence and adulthood. Attachment theory was developed from John Bowlby's observations that maternally deprived infants had an excessive need for love, which turns into demand and protest before retreating into listless withdrawal (Akhtar, 2009, p. 28). Building on Bowlby's (1977) work on pathological patterns of attachment and Henderson's (1974; 1982) identification of types of disruptive 'care eliciting behaviour' that functions to bring important others closer to the perpetrator, Adams considers that 'suicidal behaviour can more usefully be conceptualised as attachment behaviour, with its function not primarily a retreat from the world and its disappointments, but a desperate attempt to maintain relatedness to a vital attachment figure in the face of a threatening situation' (p. 15).

We agree with Adams' position that 'whatever other meanings suicidal behaviour may have it serves effectively in signalling distress to others in the social environment, admonishing them for neglect, punishing them for rejection and coercing them to re-establish a needed bond' (1985, p. 16). We believe that the revenge suicide fantasy (see p. 44 in this text) and the merging fantasy (see p. 48 in this text) represent the type of motivation for a suicide attempt described by Adams. We also agree with Adams' thinking that 'early attachment failure may lead to the persistent patterns of attachment difficulties …' (p. 16) in later life. Our understanding of the 'persistent patterns of attachment difficulties' in adolescent or adult relationships, as we explain in more detail later, is that current attachment relationships specifically, unconsciously and compulsively repeat the conflicts originally experienced with the primary caretakers of childhood. Crises in contemporary relationships are experienced as intense and overwhelming because the individual is forced to relive infantile traumas. It is the current situation which, perhaps for the first time, gives the trauma meaning and intensity.

While Adams sees the vengeful, coercive nature of some suicidal attempts as conscious reality oriented solutions to threats to current attachment relationships, we see the suicidal act as quasi-delusional, that is, one that occurs during a psychic retreat from an unbearable reality. While Adams views current interpersonal factors as the primary determinants of suicidal behaviour, we give priority to intrapsychic forces. The trigger of a suicidal act may be the perpetrator's conscious response to a contemporary crisis, but we believe that the unconscious conflicts provide the power that drives the action. We understand the suicidal act as fundamentally a solution to internalised conflicts, that is, conflicts that originated in interaction with the primary caretakers during childhood but became incorporated into the child's mind. In this way, interpersonal conflicts become intrapersonal and independent of the environment. Internalised conflicts are largely unconscious and are likely to persist even when there are positive changes in the environment. We understand the suicidal act as fundamentally a solution to internalised conflicts associated with the primary caretakers of childhood, which are largely unconscious.

This latter view is more prominent in Jeremy Holmes' chapter on suicide in his book *Exploring in Security: Towards an Attachment-Informed Psychoanalytic Psychotherapy* (2010). Holmes describes two forms of 'organised insecure attachment' as first proposed by Bowlby. The first group display 'insecure dismissive' attachment; as children these people were kept at a distance by their caregivers and as a result, as adults, they distance themselves from emotional experience and diminish its importance. After a suicide attempt they find it hard to identify the antecedent detail or what they were feeling at the time.

Holmes' second group is described as having an 'anxious clinging' attachment style; their experience in childhood was of an inconsistent caregiver whose attention they had to elicit by overactivity. As adults, they are demanding within relationships and dramatic; in contrast to the first group, their account of their suicide attempt is lengthy and circumstantial, and in therapy they seek proximity and find separation hard to bear.

Perhaps these two attachment patterns approximate to Apter's (2004) first and third groups – the schizoid narcissistic group and the depressive/neurotic group. This then poses the question, 'What of the attachment pattern of the second group?' These individuals, you will remember, are characterised as impulsive and aggressive. We would suggest that the separations and abuse in childhood has produced an 'unresolved-disorganised' pattern, which manifests features of both clinging and dismissive attachment with linguistic incoherence throughout an interview. In such individuals, negative affect is projected into those around by the acting out. It is the others, the current attachment figures, who experience the fear and distress.

Another author who considers the dynamics of the pre-suicide state of mind from an object relations point of view is Jurgen Kind in his book *Suicidal Behaviour* (1999), where he usefully considers two transitional domains. In the first transitional domain the suicidal individual's state of mind can be characterised as functioning at a pre-psychotic to borderline level in which the primary anxieties are associated with merging and keeping apart with difficulties in moving from primary to secondary process thinking, and distinguishing between the self and the other. In the second transitional domain the pre-suicide state of mind moves between borderline functioning and processes of integration, with anxieties about being able to secure the object at the manipulative, borderline end of the spectrum, which relies upon ego-syntonic splitting, to depressive states of mind where splitting is ego-dystonic and the individual is overwhelmed by guilt about aggression towards others. We

..ver a lot of the same ground as Kind, and find his way of conceptualising transitional domains complementary to our own focus on Core Complex dynamics. We are especially sympathetic with his understanding of the countertransference for colleagues working with suicidal individuals and the impact that the death by suicide of a patient has on a clinical team.

Whatever else is said about suicide, it functions as a solution born of despair and desperation. An individual enters a pre-suicide state whenever the normal self-preservative instinct, the survival of the self, is overcome and their body becomes expendable. In some cases, the patient's rejection of his or her body comes silently or may appear only indirectly in the material of therapy, but once this has occurred a suicide attempt may be made at any time.

Acting out

Suicide is a form of acting out. Freud (1914) used the term to describe the phenomenon of a patient whilst in psychoanalytic treatment who carries out an action that in symbolic form represents an unconscious wish or fantasy which cannot be experienced or expressed in any other way within the treatment. Over the years, the term has been broadened to describe a general character trait, a habitual way of being, in which a person is given to relieving any anxiety by behaviour that is self-defeating, self-harming or destructive of oneself or another.

Following Freud's (1914) paper 'Remembering, Repeating and Working Through', we view acting out is the substitute for remembering a traumatic childhood experience, and unconsciously aims to reverse that early trauma. The patient is spared the painful memory of the trauma, and via his action actively masters in the present the early experience he originally suffered passively. The actors in the current situation are seen for what they are now, rather than what they represent from the past. Furthermore, the internal drama passes directly from unconscious impulse to action, short-cutting both conscious thought and feeling. The crucial element is that the conflict is resolved (albeit temporarily) by the use of the patient's body often in a destructive or erotised way.

The person will implicate and involve others in this enactment. The others may be innocent bystanders or, as we shall see, have their own unconscious reasons for entering and playing a continuing role in the patient's scenario. The patient thus creates the characters and conflicts of his past in the people of his present, forcing them (by the use of projection and projective identification) to experience feelings which his consciousness cannot contain.

It is appropriate here to explain the terms projection and projective identification. Projection is the process whereby we resist acknowledging uncomfortable emotions within ourselves and attribute them to another person. In projective identification the recipient is unconsciously stimulated into experiencing these emotions or to enacting the projected impulse. Ogden (1984) extends the concept thus:

> Projective identification, as I understand it, allows the infant (more accurately, the mother-infant) to process experience in a way that differs qualitatively from anything that had been possible for the infant on his own. In projective identification the projector induces a feeling state in another that corresponds to a state that the projector had been unable to experience for himself. The object is enlisted in playing a role in an externalised version of the projector's unconscious state. When a recipient of a projective identification allows the induced state to reside within him without immediately attempting to rid himself of these feelings, a potential is created for the projector-recipient pair to experience that which had been projected in a manner that the projector alone had not been capable of (p. 519).

By his actions he gains temporary relief, but as the players in the patient's drama disentangle themselves from their appointed roles, projections breakdown and what has been projected returns to the patient. Because he knows no other solution by which he can escape his inner conflicts, the patient is forced to create anew the same scenario in a different setting. This is the essence of what Freud referred to as 'repetition compulsion' (Freud, 1914).

In suicide, the unconscious fantasy often revolves around settling old scores from unfinished and unacknowledged battles of childhood. These are memories that reside in that part of the patient's mind of which he is unaware and of which he has no understanding. Freud (1909) described these memories as ghosts which compulsively haunt the patient. 'That which cannot be understood inevitably reappears; like an unlaid ghost that cannot rest until the mystery has been solved and the spell broken (p. 122).

Our way into this mystery is by viewing acting out as arising from a subjective experience of physical or psychological disorder, a fantasy that finds symbolic expression in psychological phenomena or, in the case of a psychosomatic symptom, in physical illness. In acting out, it is the action that is the symbol of the unconscious conflict. As with a symptom, the exact form of the action is precisely and specifically fashioned by the unconscious fantasies and conflicts. The individual with the symptom is unlikely to be aware of the nature and function of the symptom, say a tic or self-destructive behaviour. However, another person may view the behaviour as a sign that something is not right. A close examination of the external facts of a suicidal act and the analysis of their symbolic meaning are the clearest pathway to the fantasies that have driven it.

Suicide fantasies

During a pre-suicide state the patient is influenced, in varying degrees, by different suicide fantasies, which come in combination and are based on the self's relation to its body and its primary objects (see pages 43–49). The various suicide fantasies are over-determined. The fantasies are often mutually contradictory but, being unconscious, can easily coexist. The suicidal act can be regarded as an example of a compromise formation neatly satisfying the impulses and resolving the contradictions. The suicide fantasies may or may not become conscious, but at the time of execution they have distorted reality and have the power of a delusional conviction. An illusion is 'a perception which fails to give the true character of the object perceived' (*Webster's New International Dictionary*, 1954, p. 1,242). We refer to a delusional conviction because it shares with an illusion the failure to perceive the reality of the situation, but unlike an illusion, a delusion is experienced as unshakably real. The wish to enact the suicide fantasy is the motive force. A person's promise or conscious resolve to not kill themselves, or even a strong feeling that suicide is no longer an option, does not put them beyond the risk of another attempt on their life. The suicide fantasies illuminate the conflicts that the suicidal act aims to resolve and also the wishes that self-murder gratifies. As long as the suicide fantasies are not understood and worked through, the individual is in danger of resorting to suicide as a means of dealing with conflict, pain and anxiety. For many despairing individuals, suicide is the secretly held trump card, which they are reluctant to give up because they believe, on the one hand, that it will allow them to triumph over internal adversity, and, on the other hand, to triumph over others.

The suicide fantasies are rooted in childhood and may become apparent as they are enacted in the individual's behaviour or way of relating to others. Observing and listening to a client/patient are fundamental but elusive tools which the professional can use to detect and understand suicide fantasies. We have listened to clients and patients in two contexts: 1) during a four-year period, five hundred patients were seen after admission to the casualty department of a large metropolitan teaching hospital within 24 hours of a suicide attempt (Jenkins, Hale, Papanastassiou, Crawford & Tyrer, 2002). 2) For thirty years we have listened to over fifty patients during psychoanalytic psychotherapy and psychoanalysis before and after suicide attempts. In these two groups we found that suicidal patients' fantasies about death and their affects and thoughts during the build-up to a suicide attempt confirmed Freud's earlier (1917) observation. When these patients reached the point at which they intended to kill themselves, they experienced their body as a separate object. Their attitude towards death by suicide and their suicide fantasies also confirmed Maltsberger and Buie's more recent (1980) observations and formulations of suicidal patients. While each patient expected his or her body to die, they also imagined another part of them would continue to live in a conscious bodiless state, otherwise unaffected by the death of their body. Although killing the body was an aim, it was also a means to an end. The end was the pleasurable survival of an essential part of the self, which we will refer to as the 'surviving self', a self that will survive in another dimension. This survival was dependent upon the destruction of the body (Maltsberger & Buie, 1980).

As Asch (1980) has pointed out, suicide never occurs in isolation; it is always part of a dyadic relationship, or rather its failure. One half of the dyadic relationship embodied in the suicide fantasy is the body experienced as a separate object. We think it is useful to reflect briefly on the various meanings of the word 'object'. In everyday parlance 'object' is likely to refer to 'a tangible and visible thing' (*Collins shorter English dictionary*, 1994, p. 781), which might be a person or a non-person, but is seen as an other, a not me, an external object. However, in psychoanalysis the boundary between the subject and the object, the internal and the external, is more porous, which gives rise to a variety of meanings. For our purposes we are mainly concerned with the way the subject's body can: 1) come to be perceived as an object that is separate from the self (a non-self), and 2) that the subject can split off and project unacceptable aspects of itself into this non-self body (see Klein, 1935). One consequence of this process is the breakdown of the object as a perceptually complete and emotionally balanced whole into a fragmented and unintegrated part object. The failure to distinguish between self and non-self (Stern, 1985) may lead to a breakdown in a person's orientation to reality, as in psychosis or psychotic-like states, which, we believe, occur during suicide attempts. All of this raises two critical questions for the professional: What is the nature of the object which is now identified with the body? Why is that object expendable?

References

Adams, K. S. (1985). *Early social influences on suicidal behaviour*. Paper presented at the Conference on Psychobiology of Suicidal Behaviour, New York.

Akhtar, S. (2009). *Comprehensive dictionary of psychoanalysis*. London: Karnac.

Apter, A. (2004). Personality constellations in suicidal behaviour. *Imago-Napoli Then Padova, 11*(1), 5–28.

Asch, S. S. (1980). Suicide, and the Hidden Executioner. *International Review of Psycho-Analysis, 7,* 51–60.

Bell, D. (2001). Who is killing what or whom? Some notes on the internal phenomenology of suicide. *Psychoanalytic Psychotherapy, 15*(1), 21–37. doi: 10.1080/02668730100700021

Bowlby, J. (1977). The making and breaking of affectional bonds: I. Aetiology and psychopathology in the light of attachment theory. *The British Journal of Psychiatry, 130,* 201–210. doi: 10.1192/bjp.130.3.201

Collins shorter English dictionary. (1994). Glasgow: Harper Collins.

Freud, S. (1901). The psychology of everyday life. In J. Strachey (Ed. and Trans.), *The standard edition of the complete psychological works of Sigmund Freud* (Vol. 6). London: Hogarth Press.

Freud, S. (1909). Notes on a case of obsessional neurosis. In J. Strachey (Ed. and Trans.), *The standard edition of the complete psychological works of Sigmund Freud* (Vol. 10). London: Hogarth Press.

Freud, S. (1913). Totem and taboo: Some points of agreement between the mental lives of savages and neurotic. In J. Strachey (Ed. and Trans.), *The standard edition of the complete psychological works of Sigmund Freud* (Vol. 13). London: Hogarth Press.

Freud, S. (1914). Remembering, repeating and working through. In J. Strachey (Ed. and Trans.), *The standard edition of the complete psychological works of Sigmund Freud* (Vol. 12). London: Hogarth Press.

Freud, S. ((1917)[1915]). Mourning and melancholia. In J. Strachey (Ed. and Trans.), *The standard edition of the complete psychological works of Sigmund Freud* (Vol. 14). London: Hogarth Press.

Freud, S. (1923). The Ego and the id. In J. Strachey (Ed. and Trans.), *The standard edition of the complete psychological works of Sigmund Freud* (Vol. 19). London: Hogarth Press.

Henderson, S. (1974). Care-eliciting behavior in man. *Journal of Nervous and Mental Disease, 159*(3), 172–181. doi: 10.1097/00005053-197409000-00004

Henderson, S. (1982). The significance of social relationships in the aetiology of neurosis. In C. M. Parkes & J. Stevenson (Eds.), *The place of attachment in human behaviour* (pp. 205–231). New York: Basic Books.

Holmes, J. (2010). *Exploring in security: Towards an attachment-informed psychoanalytic psychotherapy.* New York, NY US: Routledge/Taylor & Francis Group.

Jenkins, G. R., Hale, R., Papanastassiou, M., Crawford, M. J. & Tyrer, P. (2002). Suicide rate 22 years after parasuicide: Cohort study. *British Medical Journal, 325*(7373). doi: 10.1136/bmj.325.7373.1155

Kind, J. (1999). *Suicidal behaviour.* London: Jessica Kingsley.

Klein, M. (1935). A contribution to the psychogenesis of manic-depressive states. In *Love, guilt and reparation.* London: Hogarth Press.

Litman, R. E. (1996). Sigmund Freud on suicide. In J. T. Maltsberger & M. J. Goldblatt (Eds.), *Essential papers on suicide.* (pp. 200–220). New York, NY US: New York University Press. Also in *The Psychology of Suicide*, E. S. Shneidman, N. L. Farberow, and R. Litman, eds. New York: Science House, 1970, pp. 565–586.

Litman, R. E. & Swearingen, C. (1996). Bondage and suicide. In J. T. Maltsberger & M. J. Goldblatt (Eds.), *Essential papers on suicide* (pp. 243–258). New York, NY US: New York University Press.

Maltsberger, J. T. & Buie, D. H. (1980). The devices of suicide—revenge, riddance, and rebirth. *International Review of Psycho-Analysis, 7*, 61–72.

Ogden, T. H. (1984). Instinct, phantasy, and psychological deep structure: A reinterpretation of aspects of the work of Melanie Klein. *Contemporary Psychoanalysis, 20*(4), 500–525.

Stekel, W. (1910). *On suicide: With particular reference to suicide among young students* (pp. 33–141). New York: International Universities Press.

Stern, D. N. (1985). *The interpersonal world of the infant.* New York: Basic Books.

Webster's New International Dictionary. (1954). (2 ed.). Springfield, Mass., USA: CC Merriam Co.

Chapter 4

The Core Complex

The body is the original medium for the earliest communication between the mother and the infant. The satisfaction that the infant derives from its relationship with its mother will be registered in pleasurable experiences in its body, which lays the foundation for the future development of the individual's relationship with its body as a source of sensual and sexual pleasure, or confusion and anxiety. Joan Schachter's (2014) analysis of her 22-year-old patient Conrad illustrates the possible future consequences for the body when the mother's relationship with her infant does not help her child experience his or her body as a source of pleasure. Conrad did not have a sufficiently satisfying affective relationship with his mother, which left him in a state of narcissistic depletion that was often felt in his body. 'The absence of pleasurable bodily experiences which can be registered at a psychic level creates an unbridgeable gap or hole in the nascent sense of self that can only be "covered over" by the use of [the] primitive defences of splitting and projection' (Schachter, 2014, p. 29). In Conrad's case, this resulted in a negative cathexis of his body, which he attached in several suicide attempts. Schachter's study confirms our own clinical experience and the relevance of Mervin Glasser's Core Complex for understanding the pre-suicide state of mind.

From the analysis of the splitting and projection in our suicidal patients it was possible to form a general picture of an object, which, in Freud's terms, was now identified with the body, in order to understand why the body became expendable. In each case the narrative point of origin of the psychopathology (Stern, 1985) was built around a mothering object that was perceived as dangerous and untrustworthy. Separation and individuation had proved too painful for these patients and they withdrew cathexis from others while maintaining a fantasy of a regressive move to merge with an idealised mother who would meet all their needs. However, these patients felt themselves to be in a double bind. While being preoccupied with this wish to merge with mother, they become anxious about being engulfed by the object if they should succeed in merging or being abandoned to starve if they should be unsuccessful in getting into the object. Glasser (1979) identified this constellation of childhood conflicts as the Core Complex, which has proved helpful in understanding the dynamics of physical assaults on others. We believe that the Core Complex also makes a major contribution to understanding the internal conflicts which the suicide fantasy aims to resolve.

In ordinary development, the human infant is dependent upon a primary caretaker, usually the mother, for its survival. From the earliest period of development, the child develops complex and often subtle means of signalling its wishes to the mother, who usually responds appropriately to satisfy the child's needs. However, too much or too little gratification increases the child's pain, anxiety and aggression, the blame for which is defensively projected onto the mother.

When the mother is unable to accept the child's aggression and relieve his fear and pain, there are a number of consequences. The mothering object may be perceived as ungiving, poisonous or untrustworthy. The child's body, which is the medium of the mother's care, may become identified through projective identification with the bad mother or seen as the cause of her rejection. The child faced with the reality of too much or too little gratification from its mother regresses to a more primitive idealised image of an omnipotent, all-satisfying mother, with which it then tries to merge so that all his/her needs can be gratified. However, this regressive move to merge with the mother also triggers the child's anxiety about the consequences of any success in merging, namely the annihilation of its separate, independent and differentiated self. The child is now caught up in a pathological bind between the wish to satisfy its yearning to merge with the mother, on the one hand, and the fear of its own extinction if it is successful, on the other.

A threat arising from Core Complex anxieties about survival may be experienced as a direct assault, engulfment, smothering or, by contrast, abandonment to starve. The child's survival is in jeopardy. The threat of extinction mobilises ego defences in the service of preserving the self.

Ruthless and sadistic violence

Developmentally speaking, the ego's first line of defence is ruthless aggression. Threats to the infant's psychic and/or physical survival (the infant cannot be expected to know the difference between them) normally mobilise ruthless aggression directed towards the object perceived as dangerous. The aim of ruthless aggression is to negate the threat. However, when the object perceived as threatening the child's survival is the same object upon which it depends for its survival – his mother – the exercise of ruthless aggression poses a dilemma for the child. How can the infant survive the unmitigated and unmediated terror of the other? How is the child to survive if it cannot afford to get rid of mother? How can it survive the consequences of its omnipotent violence? Some children fashion an ingenious solution by libidinizing their aggression towards the mother. In this way the child changes the aim of its aggression from eliminating mother to controlling her in a libidinally gratifying way.

Ruthless aggression is, thereby, converted into sadism.

In a ruthless attack where the aim is to negate a threat (Glasser, 1979), the impact upon the object is irrelevant beyond the satisfaction of this aim. However, in a sadistic attack where the aim is to control the object by inflicting pain and suffering, the relationship to the object must be preserved, not eliminated. By radically altering the relationship to the threatening object to insure that both self and object survive, sadism now offers the child a second line of defence. This is a dominant theme in acts of self-mutilation, which we develop more fully in Chapter 10.

Subtly modulated mild sadomasochism emerges as a libidinal component of the good enough bond between mother and child. However, when the mother's sadism is not tempered by reparation or extends beyond the child's capacity to recover a nurturing image, or when mother's narcissism makes it impossible for her to be aware of her infant's needs and respond appropriately, the child may rely on more frequent and more intense sadomasochistic exchanges to control a not-good-enough mother.

Suicide fantasies will be driven by ruthless or sadistic aims in relation to the perpetrator's body and the nature of the impact of the suicidal act upon others. Most suicide fantasies represent a mixture of ruthless and sadistic suicide fantasies. However, those fantasies that aim to eliminate the body will be, on balance, more oriented to negating a threatening object (identified with the body), while revenge and punishment fantasies are more likely to be predominantly sadistic in nature. (See: types of suicide fantasies and the pre-suicide state in Chapter 5.)

Only the most disturbed people fail to negotiate the Core Complex altogether. But in suicidal adolescents and adults, we believe there may be a significant unresolved residue of the Core Complex with a specific vulnerability to acts of betrayal. We have found that suicidal individuals experience even a minor rejection or disappointment as a catastrophic blow to their self-esteem and psychic integrity, which then dramatically undercuts their capacity to cope. As psychic defences are breached, the body is felt to be at extreme risk. There follows a regressive longing to merge with the primitive omnipotent caretaker. In this state, the individual is vulnerable to re-experiencing primitive anxieties of annihilation: either being engulfed by the object if they succeed in merging, or being abandoned to starve if they are unsuccessful in getting 'into' the object.

People suffering from Core Complex anxieties in adolescent and adult relationships seem to need to hold these individuals, who represent conflicts that they experienced with their primary caregiver, at a safe distance and by specific means. To get too close to a partner raises anxieties about merging or being engulfed; to separate leaves them feeling they have been abandoned to starve. The person thus lives in a narrow corridor of safety, controlling his or her partner by acts of cruelty or coercion, never allowing the partner to make his or her own choices. Very often, the partner in the relationship will share or mirror this pathology, and thus the two become locked in mutual distrust. Normal love, consequent trust and mutuality are too dangerous, and normal modes of communication are rejected in favour of a sadomasochistic way of relating, which emphasizes control of the other.

However, when something occurs which alters the balance of the relationship, it may enter the crucial, pre-suicide phase. Whatever the event, it is seen by the potentially suicidal patient as a betrayal of a fragile truce which has held the two in equilibrium, and is perceived as a direct attack on their psychological integrity. When psychological defences are breached, the body is also felt to be at extreme risk. The at-risk individual mobilises his aggression in a psychic self-defence. His aggression may be aimed at his own body or another's.

The suicidal process

We would propose that there is a process which can be identified as the final common pathway in the majority of suicidal acts.

The starting point is that of the Core Complex – a state of equilibrium, albeit unstable. At some point an event occurs which is perceived by one partner as an act of betrayal by the other, often a disengagement or a renouncement of affection. The relationship now enters the pre-suicidal state in which the suicidal individual feels themselves to be in a vulnerable state – an accident about to happen. It may last hours or days and it is in this state that the individual consciously formulates a suicide plan and prepares the means for their own execution. Eventually, they experience the final trigger – the 'coup de grace' – described below. This propels them into a state of confusion in which they breach their own 'body barrier' and the suicidal act ensues.

This can be represented graphically thus:

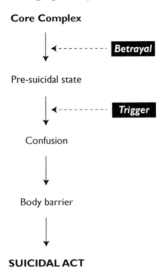

Core Complex

Pre-suicidal state

Confusion

Body barrier

SUICIDAL ACT

Figure 4.1   Progression toward a suicidal act

We understand that anxieties arising from an unresolved Core Complex leave the individual vulnerable to a catastrophic betrayal, which precipitates a pre-suicidal or pre-violent state. The path to a suicide attempt involves the trigger, the role of confusion and the body barrier.

Betrayal

The movement from the Core Complex equilibrium to the pre-suicidal state takes place when the individual experiences a specific form of betrayal which is experienced either as catastrophic abandonment or, less frequently, as humiliation. Colloquially, the suicidal individual is saying, 'All my life I have been involved in relationships which break down because partners leave me. To me, being left is to be intentionally abandoned. I thought I could trust you, but you've done it as well; so my only option is to revert to a mental state dominated by suicidal fantasies in which there is the option of enacting them.' Usually, the person cannot make this unconscious statement explicit; but it is an internal conviction.

The movement to the pre-suicidal state is not consciously recognised either, but, once entered, the person feels 'different' – as though they are on autopilot, set on a course. This state of mind may last minutes, hours or days, and it is during this period that the person is making their conscious plans for suicide – secretly preparing the means for their own execution. They are losing touch with external reality, moving into a temporary psychotic state. They are waiting for the final betrayal – the trigger, which is the final confirmation of their unconscious conviction and simultaneously the sanction for self-murder. Increasingly their actions are becoming the 'other person's' fault. The 'other person' is the partner in the long-standing sadomasochistic relationship; in its most obvious form this is a sexual partner, but it may be someone on whom the person is dependant, a superior or boss, for example.

When the individual is in therapy the therapist inevitably and necessarily becomes another person with whom the sadomasochistic relationship exists and is likely to fail them either by abandonment or humiliation.

The pre-suicide state

The Austrian psychoanalyst Erwin Ringel (1976) identified a specific state of mind that leads to suicidal acts, which he referred to as the pre-suicidal syndrome. Our conception of the pre-suicidal state of mind shares two of the three principle components proposed by Ringel, namely inhibited aggression turned against the self and suicide fantasies. The third component Ringel refers to is 'constriction', in which there is a loss of agency, breadth and flexibility, and a sense of being trapped, overpowered and helpless. Ringel views constriction as situational and dynamic. Situational constriction arises from a serious mishap, such as physical illness, or from one's own behaviour, and a subjective impression of constriction in the absence of an objectively constrictive situation. Dynamic constriction is psychologically based and is manifest in a stunted, frozen personality. There is rigidity in apperception and association, fixed patterns of behaviour and the dominance of a single affect. Time seems to stand still. Defences in which the individual himself is the object (sublimation, repression and conversion) predominate. Human relationships are depreciated and diminished in range to an attachment to a single individual or complete isolation (pp. 132–135).

Although we can see that constriction may be a component in the pre-suicide state of mind of some individuals, we do not believe, as Ringel does, that it is a necessary component. In our view, an individual enters a pre-suicide state whenever the normal self-preservative instinct is overcome and their body becomes expendable. A person may have suicidal thoughts or feel suicidal for varying lengths of time, but once the body has been rejected a suicide attempt may be made at any time (Campbell, 1995).

We agree with Ringel that the pre-suicidal syndrome, or, in our terms, the pre-suicide state, is not specific to any one type of psychopathology but is a common denominator among all suicidal individuals. The value of the concept is that it can identify danger signals, which can be used to determine when an individual is at risk of killing himself or herself. We will describe these danger signals later, but the capacity to hide or disguise the pre-suicidal state is considerable because it aims to preserve the power that the fantasies and their potential enactment give the individual. To communicate the reality of the pre-suicidal state is to renounce its power and to hand it over to the professional.

Case study: Daughter and mother

A young girl came to a casualty department with her mother having told her (correctly) that she had taken an overdose of sleeping tablets she had bought at the chemist. The girl and her mother reassured the psychiatrist and the nurses that the crisis had passed and that she would like an outpatient appointment in three days' time. Both professionals were relieved by the girl and her mother's reassurances. She went home and the day before her appointment threw herself over a high balcony. Perhaps the girl herself was at one level relieved by her own reassurances that she was not dangerous, whilst at a deeper level preserving her inner capacity for murderous enactment. In all events, no one was able to recognise the presence of the pre-suicidal state before her final suicide.

Broadly speaking there are three elements that make up the suicide attempt; the trigger, confusion and the body barrier.

The trigger

A trigger to violence or suicide may take any of three forms and precipitate the final breakdown into a destructive attack, either suicidal or violent:

1   *An actual physical attack, however small, which crosses the body boundary.* In the process of an extended argument, one workmate pushed his fingers into the ribs of Mr A to make his point more forcefully. In response, Mr A broke his mate's jaw.
2   *A physical gesture may be experienced as an attack or as rejection.* The most common gesture must be a V-sign, but it can be a denigrating look, or a turning away, or a rejection, like shutting the door in someone's face.
3   *Words which have an intrusive, dismissing and sexualised character, and are felt as a physical assault or dismissal.*

Usually, in any suicidal (or violent) attack only one of these events will provide the trigger, but what all three things have in common is, first, that they are experienced as an assault or as a rejection, and, second, that the recipient/'victim' cannot assess them objectively so that they are felt to be overwhelming. It is thus the internal meaning of the trigger that matters. What is explosive to one person may be innocuous to another. What is catastrophic at one time may be irrelevant at another.

Case study: 'Get a life'

A 26-year-old man tried to kill himself by violent means; his mother found him and prevented his death. The immediate provocation was that his mother had said, 'I do wish you would get a life of your own'. He still lived at home with his parents. When his mother was pregnant with him she unsuccessfully tried to abort him. The parents' marriage was going through a particularly troubled stage, which continued throughout his childhood such that the mother, frequently depressed, found it hard to give him the attention he needed. To the patient, therefore, his mother's statement confirmed what he had always unconsciously believed and yet not consciously known, that his existence was at his mother's expense and that he was a burden and parasite on his mother. His suicide attempt also fulfilled his mother's original wish that he should not exist.

It is interesting that the poet A. E. Housman (1939) refers to this theme in his poem specifically on suicide as, "The soul that should not have been born".

Confusion

Two observations substantiate the importance of confusion as an element in violent suicidal acts. First, in general hospitals the most common cause of violence is a toxic confusional state in which an innocuous stimulus is perceived as threatening. Delirium Tremens, a state of acute confusion in alcoholism in which individuals are often violent towards nursing staff is a good example. Second, about 35 percent of suicides, and a very large number of acts of violence, occur after alcohol has been ingested. It is commonly suggested that 'alcohol dissolves the superego' and with it the conscience and a prohibition against violence. We would also suggest that intoxication impairs the ability of the ego to discriminate between threatening and non-threatening forces whether from outside or within. As a result, terrifying conjunctions of thoughts can occur, which leaves the ego in a confusional state unable to remain separate or realistically evaluate the source of a disturbing situation.

Confusion has two elements. First, the conjunction of two previously separated ideas, probably unconscious, coming together into consciousness may be so unacceptable that they are attacked and fragmented into chaotic disorder. Second, this chaos is in itself terrifying for it represents the total loss of control that we all fear – that is, going mad. Thus, when more sophisticated ego defences fail, more primitive 'reflexive' physical defences are employed to get rid of unacceptable thoughts and feeling states. The body barrier is crossed.

Body barrier

The term body barrier describes the resistance that exists in everybody to translating the now conscious fantasy of violence into physical action. The state of confusion described above reduces this resistance. However, if this resistance has been once overcome it becomes increasingly easy to adopt a physical pathway for discharging the intra-psychic tension. This explains in part the repetitive nature of self-destructive acts.

The suicidal individual has withdrawn from others in favour of the cathexes of his own body, so that the primitive anxieties of annihilation are experienced in relation to his body that has become identified with the abandoning, humiliating or engulfing object. Violent individuals attack an external object in order to break out of an engulfing state, with the self more or less intact. A suicidal individual leaves the external object intact and assaults an internal object, represented by the body, identified with the abandoning or engulfing mother who is perceived as someone who would kill by suffocation or starvation. The body must be killed if the self is to survive. In intra-psychic terms, this is homicide, justifiable homicide. Just as there is a split between the good self and the bad body, there is a split between the hated and engulfing or abandoning primal mother, now identified with the body, and the idealised one with which the self will fuse once the bad mother's body has been eliminated.

Maltsberger (2004) provides us with an illuminating description of the phenomena of the breakdown of the ego in his paper "The descent into suicide" by commenting on the overwhelming affective states leading up to a suicidal act. He proposes a schema for self-breakdown in such states, which we quote verbatim here: 'I propose a model of suicidal collapse that involves four interlocking aspects or parts. These aspects are not to be understood as following one upon the other in strict sequence, though patients may be seen to be moving back and forth from one to another, so that shifting over time can be observed. Some patients portray one part more than another, or more than one at a time, but, as suicide nears, patients are more marked by the third and fourth parts of self-devolution. I propose the following four aspects: Aspect 1, which can be compared to flooding, finds the patient awash in an overwhelming deluge of intolerable painful feeling. This is the aspect of "affect deluge". Aspect 2, "efforts to master affective flooding", finds the patient attempting to subjugate and contain painful feeling, succeeding sometimes, sinking sometimes, and struggling, as it were, to stay afloat. When he can do this no longer, movement into the third aspect occurs, which can be likened to drowning, with the patient feeling out of control and desperate. Aspect 3 is named "loss of control and disintegration". In Aspect 4, we see the patient, his ego crippled by lost reality testing, mounting grandiose schemes for self-preservation through the jettisoning of his body. This aspect is labelled "grandiose survival and body jettison"' (p. 653–657).

The Rorschach test, which seeks to uncover unconscious motives and fantasies, has revealed interesting material that illuminates our understanding. Again, we quote Maltsberger: 'Rorschach testing can reflect loss of self-integration and failing capacity to discriminate between self and object. Inferences of such failure appear in the modes of space organisation in patient's reports of Rorschach responses, as well as in fantasies and dreams. Experiences of seeing through transparent or translucent three-dimensional spaces suggest this kind of breakdown which has been tentatively empirically associated with suicide' (Blatt & Ritzler, 1974; Roth & Blatt, 1974, as cited in Maltsberger, 2004). However, efforts at replication have raised some questions about this finding (Hansell, Lerner, Milden & Ludolph, 1988, as cited in Maltsberger, 2004).

Fowler, Piers, Hilsenroth, Holdwick & Padawer (2001, as cited in Maltsberger, 2004) developed a suicide index comprising four psychoanalytic Rorschach signs that predicted with considerable accuracy which patients would later make lethal suicide attempts. They found that 1) unconscious processes signalling penetrating affective overstimulation, 2) disturbance in capacity to maintain ego boundaries, 3) affect states characterised by morbid preoccupation with death, and 4) inner decay were strong predictors of dangerous attempts. Rydin, Åsberg, Edman & Schalling (1990) reported that violent suicide attempters were more paranoid, less able to cope with conflict situations, less able to endure dysphoric affect, and poor at differentiating between reality and imagination. These results confirm what we have described as some of the fantasies underlying suicide and the process of psychological disintegration which takes place in a suicide attempt.

A Kleinian perspective of this process would involve the gradual movement from depressive functioning (or a form of it), where there is concern for the object, to a paranoid schizoid position in which personal survival (psychic or physical) and revenge are the dominant features. After the suicidal act, assuming the patient survives, there can be a rapid return to depressive functioning with concomitant guilt for the physical damage inflicted on the body, and thus on the other person represented by the body. This process is not always recognised by either party. All too often little is resolved and the previous Core Complex equilibrium is re-established, with some degree of mutual concern. For a fuller account of a Kleinian perspective see Bell (2001).

Given that suicide takes place in the context of a dyadic relationship, or rather its failure, and that such relationships have a strong sadomasochistic character, we should give consideration to the effect of a death by suicide on the surviving partner. A study of such people reveals the relentless way that the death dominates the inner life of the survivor confirming the sadism of the original act.

Thus far we have used the words the 'dead' and the 'survivor'; perhaps a more accurate description would be the 'perpetrator' and the 'victim'. The dead person is the apparent victim, but the true victim is the one who stays alive, for s/he has to live with what s/he may feel s/he has caused. Equally, although the dead person actually carried out the act, the survivor feels that s/he, by causing it, actually perpetrated the act. Paradoxically, the dead person has achieved immortality in the survivor's mind (Pollock, 1975).

If suicide is such a singular form of death, it follows that it will need a different and equally singular form of mourning. Is such a process possible? How can you mourn for someone whose death you felt you were in part responsible for by your own sadism and as a result of which part of you was killed? It seems as though the act of suicide freezes the relationship at the zenith of its sadism, and that the survivor erects enormous resistances to any change or working through of this state, almost as a memorial to the dead (Barnett & Hale, 1985).

Nonetheless, many people bereaved by suicide frequently seek psychotherapeutic help and perhaps there are no universal solutions; each person will find their own way of understanding, explaining or rationalising these incredibly painful events so they can live in their aftermath.

References

Barnett, B. & Hale, R. (1985). *A singular form of death: Some aspects of the psychological sequelae of the loss of the father by suicide.* Paper presented at the Congress of the International Psychoanalytical Association, Hamburg.

Bell, D. (2001). Who is killing what or whom? Some notes on the internal phenomenology of suicide. *Psychoanalytic Psychotherapy, 15*(1), 21–37. doi: 10.1080/02668730100700021

Campbell, D. (1995). The role of the father in a pre-suicide state. *The International Journal of Psychoanalysis, 76*(2), 315–323.

Glasser, M. (1979). Some aspects in the role of aggression in the perversions. In I. Rosen (Ed.), *Sexual Deviations* (Vol. 2, pp. 278–305). Oxford: Oxford University Press.

Housman, A. E. (1939). *The collected poems of A. E. Housman.* London: Penguin Books.

Maltsberger, J. T. (2004). The descent into suicide. *The International Journal of Psychoanalysis, 85*(3), 653–668. doi: 10.1516/3C96-URET-TLWX-6LWU

Pollock, G. H. (1975). On mourning, immortality, and utopia. *Journal of the American Psychoanalytic Association, 23*, 334–362.

Ringel, E. (1976). The pre-suicidal syndrome. *Suicide and Life-Threatening Behaviour, 6*(3), 131–149.

Rydin, E., Åsberg, M., Edman, G. & Schalling, D. (1990). Violent and nonviolent suicide attempts: A controlled Rorschach study. *Acta Psychiatrica Scandinavica, 82*(1), 30–39. doi: 10.1111/j.1600-0447.1990.tb01351.x

Schachter, J. (2014) 'Seized with a savage woe': Attacks on the vitality of the body in a suicidal young man. In *The Bulletin of the British Psychoanalytical Society*, 50: 9, November 2014, 22–30.

Stern, D. N. (1985). *The interpersonal world of the infant.* New York: Basic Books.

Chapter 5

Suicide fantasies and the pre-suicide state of mind

During a pre-suicide state the patient is influenced, in varying degrees, by a suicide fantasy which reflects the self's relation to its body and an other. The fantasy may or may not become conscious, but at the time of execution it has the power of a delusion conviction and has distorted reality. The suicide fantasy is the motive force. Killing the body fulfils the fantasy (Campbell & Hale, 1991).

Ringel (1976) notes the imminent danger of suicide when active or passive suicidal fantasies, which occur without wilful intention, shift into deliberate passive-compulsive suicide notions. We emphasise the value of understanding the nature and functions of an individual's suicide fantasy because their answer to the question: 'Do you intend to commit suicide?' is unreliable and should not, on its own, be used to downgrade the risk of suicide. Needless to say, feelings of guilt and shame, the need to protect suicide as an escape or solution, or the power of repression make it difficult to discover suicide fantasies. We concur with Ringel that questions about dreams are more likely to be answered truthfully than those about suicide fantasies (p.149).

Ringel differentiated three stages of increasing danger in suicide fantasies: 1) Imagining being dead. It is usually easier to imagine being dead than to think about dying, especially since being dead is often experienced as a new form of continual life. He links this to a regression into childhood fantasies where death is a reversible phenomenon. 2) The notion of committing suicide without a specific plan. 3) Specific suicide plans, frequently in minute detail (p. 138).

We hold the view that those suicide fantasies, which elaborate the relationship between the 'surviving self' and the body, take at least five forms, which will be described briefly. Although one type of fantasy may dominate consciousness, suicide fantasies are interdependent and at an unconscious level not mutually exclusive. Within the patient, each fantasy is organised around a wish to gratify pre-genital impulses, which are predominantly sadomasochistic or oral-incorporative in nature.

First, an almost universal suicidal fantasy is the *revenge fantasy*. The revenge fantasy centres on the impact that the suicide makes on others. Here, a conscious link to a real object is maintained more strongly than in other suicide fantasies. The frequent conscious thought in the revenge fantasy is, 'They will be sorry'. The implicit message is that the parents have raised a child who hates himself because they did not love him enough. The threat of suicide to blackmail others may accompany the revenge fantasy. Zilborg (1936; 1996) emphasised the spite which motivates some suicides. He also suggests that primal scene experiences may promote suicidality. This view is supported by Perelberg (1999) who has observed that primal scene scenarios are motivating factors in violence towards others.

This suicide fantasy has a markedly sadistic orientation, with the surviving self often enjoying the role of the invisible observer of others' suffering, especially due to their feelings of guilt and remorse because of the suicide. There is a sense of retaliation, revenge and irrevocable, everlasting triumph.

Case study: A revenge fantasy

A young girl was seen the day after a suicide attempt. Towards the end of his assessment the examining psychiatrist asked her what she wanted to do now, expecting her to say, 'I want to go to be with my mum, or my aunt or my best friend.' Instead, she replied, 'I want to go to a very high building and throw myself off on to a concrete car park and know that my mum is watching when I hit the ground.'

A second fantasy, the *self-punishment fantasy*, is dominated by guilt, frequently associated with masturbation which aims to gratify, in fantasy, incestuous wishes, and an erotisation of pain and death or complicity in sexual abuse. Here, the surviving self is gratified by its sadistic treatment of its own body rather than that of others, as occurs in a revenge fantasy.

Masochistic impulses are satisfied as well, in the self's identification with the helpless, passive, submissive body.

Case study: Self-punishment fantasy and eroticisation in a completed suicide

This sadomasochistic dynamic is evident in the complexity of those sexually deviant practices that maintain a delicate balance between masochistic pleasure in self-torture and the risk of death, as in the dicing-with-death phenomenon (described later), and is illustrated by the suicide of a man who had broken off treatment two years prior to his death.

He was found hanged above a fallen chair and dressed only in a raincoat surrounded by burning candles. From the patient's earlier accounts of his elaborate ritual, it was clear that the 'surviving self' in his suicide fantasy was secretly identified with Joan of Arc, a woman who victoriously led men in battle and was martyred and reincarnated in a new dimension as a saint.

By using understanding of the patient's unconscious wishes from his previous therapy, we can speculate that underlying the risk-taking, sadomasochistic dynamic was an infantile wish to get inside a woman; he was naked inside the raincoat, thereby sharing her death. The sacrifice of his male body was the means to that end. The candles represented her execution pyre; the noose introduced excitement with the real risk of death. This tragic and extreme case illustrates the interplay between sadomasochistic and oral incorporative impulses and the coexistence of one or more fantasies during a pre-suicidal state.

This patient is an example of an unusual but not uncommon suicide in the context of bondage and fetishistic masturbation. Litman (1970), and Litman and Swearingen (1996), who have written about this phenomenon, note the way self-destruction is moderated by ritual and sublimation in masturbation and defended against by perversion. This case is also an example of the role that a dicing-with-death dynamic (see pages 47 and 74 in our text) plays in suicide. It appears that when dicing with death is part of an autoerotic bondage it is more likely to result in death (suicide) than bondage involving a partner. Our experience confirms Litman and Swearingen's view that 'the essential element that these men had in common was the eroticisation of a situation of helplessness, weakness, and threat to life which was then overcome in survival, and there was eventual triumph' (p. 254). However, the element of a real danger of death is necessary in order to validate the triumph of survival.

This interplay of fantasies is particularly remarkable during the turbulent, fluctuating time of adolescence. Adolescents who are dominated by pre-genital needs and have had difficulty in separating from their parents may blame their sexual bodies for the incestuous guilt they feel over intrusive wishes. These adolescents believe that punishment of their body by killing it is the only way to relieve them of their guilt. (This will be developed further in Chapter 8: Pre-suicide states in adolescence.)

A third fantasy is the assassination fantasy. In the assassination fantasy, which is seen particularly in adolescence, there are similar conflicts between pubertal sexuality and the unresolved pre-Oedipal needs. Laufer and Laufer (1984) have drawn attention to the way in which adolescents, as well as adults, may experience their bodies as a source of madness when unacceptable regressive infantile wishes are felt to be located in their sexually maturing body, which then seems confusing, alien and threatening. The self in their suicide fantasies 'survives', paradoxically, by killing a body that is driving them mad. Although there are likely to be sadomasochistic aspects, the predominant feeling is relief that a threat has been disposed of, as a violent individual feels after beating off what he believed to be an attack on his life.

In the assassination fantasy, the body is experienced as a destroyer. In some cases, it threatens to destroy sanity, while in other cases the body threatens to kill the self. The mechanism is similar to that seen in paranoid cases, with its reliance upon splitting aspects of the self and projecting them into others. But for the suicidal patient with an elimination fantasy, a split-off body is the object upon which is projected murderous impulses in such a way that the 'me' self then feels that its 'not me' body is occupied by an assassin (Maltsberger & Buie, 1980).

What distinguishes this suicide fantasy from others is that the surviving self is motivated less by malicious intent, as in the revenge and punishment fantasies, than by primitive self-preservative instincts. The body is not an object of sadistic attack by the self, nor is the self preoccupied with revenge upon others.

The internal dynamics are similar to those of the individual who feels ensnared in the Core Complex to the extent that he believes his life is at risk and reacts with ruthless violence. In the psychotic life and death struggle contained in the assassination fantasy, the only thing that matters to the surviving self is the elimination of the killer body to avoid total annihilation. In this fantasy, suicide is conceived of as killing the assassin body before it kills the self. Suicide is enacted in self-defence.

Case study: An assassination

A 19-year-old boy was tortured by unacceptable perverse fantasies during a pre-suicide state. In a session, as the tension created by suicidal thoughts reached the breaking point, he shouted, 'I have got these thoughts. Up here. (He tapped the top of his head.) I can't get rid of them. They are driving me mad. I just want to get a gun, put it right here. (He pushed his index finger into the top of his head.) And blast them out. POW!'

We believe that the assassination fantasy is predominate when suicide occurs in the context of what, in descriptive psychiatric terms, would be regarded as a paranoid psychotic (or schizophrenic) state.

The assassination fantasy should be distinguished from the purification fantasy, which predominates in acts of self-mutilation, and is characterized by 'delusion' or unconscious belief that the body is infested or infected by some toxic substance (often as a result of sexual abuse), which the cutting or burning will remove.

A fourth fantasy is the dicing-with-death fantasy. The patient who is compelled to dice with death actively puts his body, or a symbolic representative of it, at risk in order to both attract and attack the primary object. This may take obvious forms, such as compulsive gambling or driving whilst drunk. It may be structured and socially sanctioned in activities such as parachuting and mountaineering or motor racing, or involve various kinds of delinquency and sexual deviancy. Whatever the risk-taking activity, it should alert the clinician to the fact that the patient may enter a pre-suicide state, and careful attention should be given to the fantasies which are being gratified. Obviously, many risk-takers do not lose touch with reality and do not exceed the limits of their bodies, their equipment or their environment. Nevertheless, because they maintain a delicate balance between failure and triumph, changes in their internal state can alter that balance with fatal results.

Case study: The reckless driver

A patient who had numerous car accidents assumed that others should look out for him. He saw no need to drive within speed limits. He was, in Freud's terms, 'the exception'; that is, someone who had unjustly suffered enough as a child and felt he had a right to a fantasised mother he had never had – an omnipotent mother represented by fate and other drivers who would anticipate his behaviour and protect him from any danger. By putting himself at risk, he hoped to arouse anxiety in others, especially his analyst, and provoke them to rescue him and make him safe and secure. But this attitude towards his body, a body that he did not value enough to protect, represented an identification with the neglectful mother, as well as his condemnation of her. There is a strong sadomasochistic dynamic in both passive submission to fate, on the one hand, and actively flaunting the risk-taking, on the other.

The role of fate is well described by Asch (1980), who compares this aspect of suicide to Russian roulette: 'The power of life or death, the role of the executioner, is thrust onto fate with the implicit thought, "I will force fate to make the choice between bullet or empty chamber for me." Or, in the arena more familiar to our profession, fate is forced to decide if the patient will be found before his sleeping pills take their lethal effect. It becomes clear that fate will be forced to embrace his victim and accept the executioner's role'.

The fifth suicide fantasy underpinning all of the other fantasies is a merging fantasy. In 1940 Hendrick (1996) observed that fusion with a lost primary object was the fundamental aim of suicide. However, the merging fantasy may be represented by substitutes for the primary object of infanthood. For instance, patients who harbour a merging suicidal fantasy may imagine death as a return to nature, becoming one with the universe, achieving a state of nothingness or a permanent sense of peace, a passport into a new world, or a blissful dreamless eternal sleep. Friedlander (1996) noted that in 'the longing to die' the unconscious inextricably links the wish to die with the wish to sleep. The patients believe that in death the self will survive in a state akin to that of the sleeping infant. The dominant wish is to be fused 'with the image of the Madonna of infancy. By becoming one with her, the suicidal patient hopes to taste again the omnipotent, timeless, mindless peace of his baby origins, far from the wearisome hostile inner presence of his miserable adulthood' (Maltsberger & Buie, 1980, p. 67).

However, as seen in the Core Complex, the wish to fuse with an omnipotent mother is accompanied by an anxiety about the consequences of fulfilling that wish, the annihilation of the self. In the psychotic state typical of those dominated by suicidal fantasies, splitting of the self from the body leaves these patients believing that the body is actually an impediment to the fulfilling of the merging fantasy. The body is identified with the engulfing or abandoning mother and is then eliminated. Once the body is eliminated the 'surviving self' is free to fuse with the idealised Madonna-mother of infancy.

Although there are different types of suicide fantasies (see Maltsberger & Buie, 1980; Campbell & Hale, 1991) each fantasy is underpinned by a wish for the 'surviving self' to merge with an idealised maternal imago. The suicide fantasy represented a solution to the conflict, which resulted from the wish to merge with mother, on the one hand, and the consequent primitive anxieties about annihilation of the self, on the other. By projecting the hated, engulfing or abandoning primal mother onto the body and then killing it, the surviving self was free to fuse with the split-off idealised, desexualised, omnipotently gratifying mother represented by states of oceanic bliss, dreamless eternal sleep, a permanent sense of peace, becoming one with the universe, or achieving a state of nothingness (Maltsberger & Buie, 1980).

Just as there was a split between the good 'surviving self' and the bad body, there was also a split between the hated, engulfing or abandoning primal mother, now identified with the body, and the idealised one with which the 'surviving self' would safely fuse once the bad mother/body had been eliminated.

References

Asch, S. S. (1980). Suicide, and the hidden executioner. *International Review of Psycho-Analysis, 7*, 51–60.

Campbell, D. & Hale, R. (1991). *Suicidal acts*. London: Churchill Livingstone.

Friedlander, K. (1996). On the 'longing to die'. In J. T. Maltsberger & M. J. Goldblatt (Eds.), *Essential papers on suicide*. (pp. 93–103). New York, NY US: New York University Press.

Hendrick, I. (1996). Suicide as wish fulfillment. In J. T. Maltsberger & M. J. Goldblatt (Eds.), *Essential papers on suicide*. (pp. 104–117). New York, NY US: New York University Press.

Laufer, M. & Laufer, M. E. (1984). *Adolescence and developmental breakdown: A psychoanalytic view*. New Haven, CT US: Yale University Press.

Litman, R. E. (1970). Sigmund Freud on suicide. In J. T. Maltsberger & M. J. Goldblatt (Eds.), *Essential papers on suicide*. (pp. 200–220). New York, NY US: New York University Press.

Litman, R. E. & Swearingen, C. (1996). Bondage and suicide. In J. T. Maltsberger & M. J. Goldblatt (Eds.), *Essential papers on suicide*. (pp. 243–258). New York, NY US: New York University Press.

Maltsberger, J. T. & Buie, D. H. (1980). The devices of suicide—revenge, riddance, and rebirth. *International Review of Psycho-Analysis, 7*, 61–72.

Perelberg, R. J. (1999). *Psychoanalytic understanding of violence and suicide*. London: Routeledge.

Ringel, E. (1976). The pre-suicidal syndrome. *Suicide and Life-Threatening Behaviour,* 6(3), 131–149.

Zilborg, G. (1936). Differential diagnostic types of suicide. *Archives of General Psychiatry, 35,* 270–291.

Zilborg, G. (1996). Differential diagnostic types of suicide. In J. T. Maltsberger, & M. J. Goldblatt, *Essential papers on suicide* (pp. 36–61). New York: New York University Press.

Chapter 6

How learning from the patient generates theory

Listening to a patient in a pre-suicide state is easier said than done. For the professional it often feels like working in the dark. However, if we do not give up on our patients or ourselves, we can learn about what makes it difficult to listen to a particular client and, most importantly, how that difficulty is related to their pre-suicide state. Sadly, at times we have to learn from our mistakes. Mr Adams is a case in point.

Case study: Material from Donald Campbell's analysis of Mr Adams[1]

Mr Adams was a 'mummy's boy', who was alternately indulged and abandoned according to the whims of his narcissistic mother. He felt rejected by his father who was seldom at home and appeared to favour his older brother. Mr Adams wanted to join in the family business after A-Levels and was hurt when father sent him off to university in Glasgow. His father died of cancer shortly after Mr Adams returned to Edinburgh with his degree. At the age of 30, while under severe stress at work, Mr Adams took an overdose of Valium. Believing it to be potentially lethal. A year later, on the brink of a business failure, he took another overdose and cut his wrists.

When he was 40, Mr Adams came to see me looking dishevelled and unshaven after he had gambled away all of his money – half a million pounds. He looked and sounded melancholic – feeling impoverished (as he was in reality), slighted and unjustly treated. He told me that when he went to a casino he often started with a little money but soon won thousands, only to lose it all at the end of the night. (It is interesting that compulsive gamblers often say that they only feel safe when they have lost all their money – perhaps in fear of an Oedipal triumph.) His older brother had taken over his financial affairs, blocked all of his bank accounts, left him with a weekly allowance and went off to Japan for a holiday. Mr Adams said that he felt suicidal and then made a slip, saying 'father' instead of 'brother' had left him and gone off to Japan. When I called his attention to his slip he referred to his suicidal thoughts and added, 'it all started with my father's death'.

After Mr Adams' father died, his mother confided only in him that she would one day commit suicide. In passing, he said that his mother also confided to him that she had 'killed' her own mother with a drug overdose after she had a paralysing stroke. After associating to his fear that his wife might leave him, Mr Adams added that he didn't understand why he always avoided his mother.

One month after Mr Adams started five times weekly analysis, his mother made a serious but unsuccessful suicide attempt at home in Edinburgh. Mr Adams wasn't surprised. 'I didn't go to see her because my brother is there. I'm glad he's upset and had to come back from Tokyo. I stayed in bed all day yesterday.' Mr Adams justified his coldness by referring to his family's very rational attitude to death. Without recognising the failure of this defence, he described his father as 'paranoid, full of fear and panic during his last week. His face at the undertaker's was distorted and ugly. I tried to push his lips into a calm expression. My mother is always calm'.

The next day he was furious that his brother advised him not to sell his shares to settle his debts, but to keep them and gamble that they would increase in value. I linked his rage at being put at risk to satisfy his brother's wish for excitement with his mother's secret which had put him at risk as the passive, guilty accomplice, waiting for a predicted self-murder. I then took up what I thought was his fear that I would put him at risk by not taking seriously his earlier attempts to kill himself.

In the sessions, Mr Adams regularly complained that I did not give him advice and suggestions. I interpreted this behaviour in the transference in terms of his view of me as distant and withdrawn and his efforts to get compensation for what his mother failed to give him by actively demanding more from me. This was often followed by transient regressed states featuring rambling and mumbled conversation and narcissistic withdrawal into drowsiness, which I interpreted as Mr Adams' identification with his narcissistic mother. This appeared to be what Pearl King (1978) refers to as a reverse transference, that is the patient relating to the analyst in such a way to give the analyst the experience of the patient as a child by relating to the analyst as the parent had done. My interpretations seemed to have a positive effect and there were obvious signs of improvement in Mr Adams's appearance.

Mr Adams's gambling represented a manic solution to his feelings of helplessness, impotence and despair. I understood the self-defeating, self-impoverishing aspect of his gambling behaviour as Mr Adams dicing with death, particularly after his mother's suicide attempt increased his anxiety about his own survival. I was worried about the self-destructive component of his gambling. As his wish to triumph over the odds intensified, I took up his pattern of losing money as a way of demonstrating his mother's failure by leaving him bereft and without resources. His failures also invited his mother to rescue him and it was now clear he wanted me to do the same. These interpretations also appeared to have an effect; Mr Adams stopped gambling. Furthermore, his attitude became more positive and he began investing again in his work and family.

At this point, Mr Adams interrupted his analysis in an optimistic frame of mind to go to Edinburgh, his hometown, to try to generate business for his neglected company. However, once there business did not go well and he couldn't face his old friends.

On a Sunday afternoon he felt lonely and suicidal and called his wife in London, hoping she would express sympathy and come to join him. Instead, Mrs Adams complained about his using suicide to blackmail her. She couldn't stand his threats anymore and told him to get on with it if he was going to kill himself.

At first Mr Adams felt shattered, hurt, rejected and totally alone. However, once he decided to kill himself he felt great relief and calm. He took seventy 10 mg tablets of Valium in the belief that would be enough to kill him and lay down feeling at peace. As the pills took effect he felt he was drifting off into another dimension. There was a sense of oneness, a merging into another kind of existence. He was found by accident and rushed to hospital in time. Although Valium, even in a large overdose, is not pharmacologically lethal, a fact of which Mr Adams was unaware, it is the lethality of the intent which is important. (It is also relevant that the most common drugs taken in overdose are either analgesics – pain killers – or psychotropic medication – psychic painkillers. Moreover, it has recently been established that both physical pain and psychological pain stimulate the same part of the brain.)

I was shocked when I heard the news. I felt that I had missed something and had let Mr Adams down.

Let us now consider what the analyst learned from Mr Adams after his suicide attempt, what the analyst learned by thinking again about what Mr Adams had told the analyst before the attempt, and compare this with other suicidal patients.

Countertransference during a pre-suicide state

The assessment of Mr Adams' suicide attempt began with the fact that the analyst was shocked when he heard the news. He assumed that understanding this response would shed some light on why he was caught by surprise.

Sandler's (1976) concept of the analyst's role response provided a useful framework for considering the analyst's reaction. Sandler draws attention to the patient's unconscious attempts to provoke the analyst to behave in such a way as to confirm the patient's illusory (transference) image of the analyst. The analyst may hold his response to this prodding in his consciousness (King (1978) referred to this as his 'affective response') and make use of it to understand the transference. Failure to hold responses and the enactment of them in behaviour, attitude or remark represents the analyst's unconscious role response. Sandler suggests that 'very often the irrational response of the analyst, which his professional conscience leads him to see entirely as a blind spot of his own, may sometimes be usefully regarded as a compromise-formation between his own tendencies and his reflexive acceptance of the role which the patient is forcing on him' (Sandler, 1976, p. 46).

Sandler views this type of countertransference reaction as a piece of behaviour or an attitude that results from the overlap of the patient's pathology and the analyst's. Consequently, the professional is only likely to become aware of his role in a countertransference interaction by observing his own feelings and behaviour after the fact, after he has responded. Nevertheless, by viewing his countertransference behaviour as related to the patient, and thinking of it as a compromise between his own tendencies or propensities and the role relationship, which the patient is unconsciously seeking to elicit, the analyst can deepen his understanding of the transference and his part in the patient's suicide scenario.

It became apparent that an essential ingredient of the pre-suicide state is the patient's attempt to involve the analyst in an active way in the suicide scenario. Straker (1958) pointed out, 'A decisive factor in the successful suicide attempt appears to be the implied consent or unconscious collusion between the patient and the person most involved in the psychic struggle' (p. 479). The unconscious collusion is buried in the analyst's countertransference.

Asch (1980) has demonstrated the vulnerability that the therapist of the suicidal patient has to being provoked into negative countertransference attitudes, which are experienced by the patient as collusion in the suicidal fantasy. This collusion confirms for the patient the analyst's active participation in a regressive sadomasochistic fusion, places the analyst in the role of the executioner, and gives the patient justification for retaliation via a suicide attempt.

Relevant here is the journalist Andrew Tyler's (1990) account given in the *London Evening Standard* of the impact on London Underground train drivers when they have the experience of someone throwing themselves under their train. Worse still is when the 'jumper' catches the driver's eye as they throw themselves off the platform. But the worst effect is when they catch his or her eye and smile. For the drivers it is as though the suicidal individual has appointed them as an innocent and unwitting executioner who has been forced to become complicit in an act of extreme sadomasochism. Not surprisingly, the drivers experience all the symptoms of post-traumatic stress disorder, with some unable to return to train driving.

The sadomasochistic dynamic may also manifest itself in the subtle, superficially benign form of the patient's feeling of being at peace, which contributes to increased self-assurance and confidence (Laufer & Laufer, 1984). Depressive affects, anxieties and conflicts are no longer communicated. This narcissistic withdrawal cuts the therapist off from moods and behaviour, which would normally elicit an empathic response of alarm or worry and may result in the sudden loss of subjective emotional concern (Tahka, 1978) for the patient.

In a narcissistic regression, which dominated our patients during the pre-suicide state, there is the prospect of imminently fulfilling a merging suicide fantasy. As far as these patients were concerned, they were already at peace because they had crossed a rational barrier of self-preservation, identified the assassin/mother with their body, and had no doubts about killing it.

The professional, burdened with anxieties about his or her patient's life or exhausted by the patient's relentless attack on hope or angry about being blackmailed (often before a holiday break from treatment), may be tempted to retaliate by giving up on his or her patient, or use the patient's sense of peace to justify relaxing his therapeutic vigilance. In the case of Mr Adams, external signs of decreased stress and improvement in the patient were used by the analyst to defend against the analyst's unconscious wishes to retaliate by letting go of the suicide risk.

Note

1   This case study is taken from Campbell & Hale (1991) and Campbell (1995).

References

Asch, S. S. (1980). Suicide, and the hidden executioner. *International Review of Psycho-Analysis, 7*, 51–60.

Campbell, D. (1995) The role of the father in a pre-suicide state. *International Journal of Psychoanalysis, 76*, 315–323.

Campbell, D. & Hale, R. (1991) Suicidal acts. In J. Holmes (Ed.), *Textbook of psychotherapy in psychiatric practice*, (pp. 287–306). London: Churchill Livingstone.

King, P. (1978). Affective response of the analyst to the patient's communications. *The International Journal of Psychoanalysis, 59*(2–3), 329–334.

Laufer, M. & Laufer, M. E. (1984). *Adolescence and developmental breakdown: A psychoanalytic view*. New Haven, CT US: Yale University Press.

Sandler, J. (1976). Countertransference and role-reponsiveness. *International Review of Psycho-Analysis, 3*, 43–78.

Straker, M. (1958). Clinical observations of suicide. *Canadian Medical Association Journal, 79*, 473–479.

Tahka, V. A. (1978). On some narcissistic aspect of self-destructive behaviour and their influence on its predicatability. *Psychiatra Fennica Supplementum*, 59–62.

Tyler, A. (1990, November). Blood on the tracks. *The Evening Standard*, pp. 44–49.

Chapter 7

The role of the father in the pre-suicide state[1]

The questions for the analyst of Mr Adams remain. 'Who was I in the transference? Who was the object evoked by Mr Adams and enacted by me?' It was clear from Mr Adams that he felt distant and alienated from his father. The absence of his father in Mr Adams' material was consistent with their relationship. The analyst's failure to perceive and respond interpretatively to Mr Adams' suicide risk confirmed his role as the distant, uninvolved father. Mr Adams gave the impression that his father had failed his son during an early phase of development.

In normal development, both pre-Oedipal parents represent to the child the world outside the exclusivity of the mother-infant relationship, e.g. the realities of time and place and objects. So far our focus has been on the dyadic relationship of the mother and child. Now we will consider the role that the 'good-enough' pre-Oedipal father plays as friendly rival with both his child and his wife, in offering each of them a dyadic relationship that is parallel to and competes with the mother-child unit.

In 'good-enough' fathers the pleasure of procreation and the birth of his child is accompanied by feelings of envy and exclusion from the mother-child relationship as well as adjustment to a secondary role with the child. Initially, fathers can defend against this change by supporting the mother and making use of passive feminine aspects of their makeup to identify with the mother. However, a more active, masculine identification will emerge in the father's relationship with his child and wife. The attractive and attracting father stakes a claim on his child and, with mother's help, enables the child to move from the exclusivity of the infant-mother relationship into an inclusive position as part of a pre-Oedipal triad.

Father's gender role identity and parental Oedipal impulses influence the idiosyncratic nature of the claim he makes on his child. For instance, his conscious and unconscious fantasies and anxieties about female sexuality will affect the way he relates to his daughter from the beginning. She may be 'daddy's little girl'. Father's anxieties about femininity may also influence the way he views his wife's relationship with his son. The father may even be conscious of not wanting his wife to 'feminise' his son. He may worry that she will make his son 'soft', or turn him into a 'sissy'. Gender-influenced relating will also play a part in the way a father helps his son dis-identify from mother (Greenson,1968). In ordinary development the child identifies with its first object of attachment – a maternal figure, the mother or her representative. When the child is a boy he usually moves away from an identification with a maternal figure to identify with a masculine person who shares the boy's gender. This move requires an additional task for the boy, one that the little girl does not need to go through, namely to dis-identify from mother, in order to identify with father. Boys who are raised by mothers in single-parent families will look for other males to identify with and especially the way the mother values men and relates to them.

Whatever form this process of claiming his child takes, and there will always be infinite variations influenced by mixtures of projections and reality, the child will become aware that he or she occupies a place in father's mind that is separate and distinct from mother.

The child also becomes aware of a place for mother in father's mind and a place for father in mother's mind. Father reclaims his wife by 'drawing' her back to him and rekindling her adult sexuality. The father who reclaims his wife and engages his child on his own terms protects them both from lingering overlong in a 'fusional' or symbiotic state and facilitates the separation and individuation process (Mahler & Gosliner, 1955).

Freud (1931) recognised the little girl's attachment to her father as a refuge from her first attachment to mother. Loewald (1951) referred to the child's positive, pre-Oedipal relationship with the father who stands for a paternal veto against the engulfing and overpowering womb that threatens to undermine the ego's orientation to reality and its efforts to establish boundaries between self and other.

The father's twofold response supports the child's right to an independent existence that is separate from mother while providing the toddler with a means of coping with its longing for her. Abelin (1978) postulates that around eighteen months this process results in an early triangulation in which the toddler identifies with the rival father's wish for mother to form a mental representation of a self that is separate and longing for mother. The good-enough father provides a model for identification as well as an alternative relationship to the child's regressive wish to return to a 'fusional' state with mother with subsequent anxieties about engulfment.

In the analysis of suicidal patients it often becomes apparent that they perceived their fathers as either withdrawn or actively rejecting them, and as having failed to reclaim their wives. Each patient had felt abandoned to his or her anxieties about surviving as a differentiated self when left with a disturbed mother.

As we will emphasise in Chapter 8, 'Pre-suicide states in adolescence', when the boy is unable to identify with his father in a way that supports his masculine identity, the boy may encounter difficulties in separating from his mother and establishing a separate and independent existence. The Oedipal girl is faced with a different task, namely, to change the object of desire from mother to father. In so doing, her link to the primary object is severed with the resultant anxieties of separation and retaliation.

The patients' suicide fantasies articulated in the present represented internalised early pathological relationships between mother and child and father. The pre-Oedipal father's role was often obscured by the patient's relationship with the mother, which dominated the suicide fantasy, and by the father's absence or ineffectiveness. However, it was during the pre-suicide state that the internalised father's failure to intervene in the pathological mother/child relationship became most critical.

It was clear that Mr Adams intended to kill his body while maintaining the fantasy that part of him would survive. After taking the overdose, Mr Adams felt calm as he had described his mother and expected to pass into 'another dimension', wondering what it would be like.

There was evidence of the coexistence of other suicide fantasies. Mr Adams' suicide attempt was influenced by his identification with his suicidal mother. For instance, while talking about his suicide attempt he made a slip saying his mother was 40 – his age. It also emerged in his analysis that Mr Adams hoped that his suicide would serve as revenge against both his parents.

Mr Adams' suicide fantasies were organised around a sadomasochistic relationship with his mother, whose shared secret had tortured him by making him an accomplice in a homicide (the overdose that she had administered to her own mother) and her own planned suicide. His mother's unsuccessful attempt on her life increased his guilt because he had ignored her explicit warnings that she would kill herself. His fear that she would kill him increased as well. He slipped in telling the analyst of his mother's suicide attempt, saying, 'My mother tried to kill myself'.

Mr Adams felt his father did not relate to him in his own right. For instance, father could not support his son's wish to join him in the family business. Mr Adams associated feeling suicidal to being left by his father, and then recalled that his suicidal fantasies started with his father's death. However, Mr Adams felt abandoned to his mother by his father long before his father's death. Father and brother had paired off while he was left with mother. Without his father as an alternative object with whom to identify, Mr Adams was left in a masochistic tie to a murderous mother.

Although Mr Adams' suicide fantasies were primarily the outcomes of a pathological bond with his mother, during the pre-suicide state his relationship with his father, particularly father's failure to protect him from his mother, functioned as the sanction of the suicidal act.

Mr Adams relied upon splitting of the self and the object to survive his mother's suicide attempt, which he experienced as an attack on his life. The resulting suicide fantasy during the pre-suicide state had two components: an unconscious fantasy and a delusional conviction. Mr Adams' unconscious fantasy that identified his body with a bad mother initially came into the analysis as nonverbal communications in his neglect and mistreatment of his body. After his suicide attempt, this identification was put into words by Mr Adams: 'Mother couldn't care for her body and she couldn't care for mine. How could I care for myself?' Getting rid of his bad mother, now identified with the object of his suicidal attack – his body – would make it possible for his split-off surviving self to merge with the split-off idealised mother – the nameless 'other dimension'.

There was a breakthrough of his unconscious identification of his body with his mother and his sadistic revenge against the bad mother, represented by his wife, when he made a slip: 'I can't say to my wife "I want to kill yourself."' The fantasy of merging with an idealised mother (which was on his mind when he took the pills) became a delusional conviction during the pre-suicide state.

Mr Adams' slip of the tongue, 'My mother tried to kill myself', represented a breakthrough of a preconscious awareness of mother's sadistic attack on him via her suicide attempt and formed the basis of his identification with the aggressor. In proceeding with his suicide plan Mr Adams turned passive into active, and shifted from a masochistic to a sadistic role in order to extract revenge. Mr Adams' depression lifted as he planned the details of his execution, which included collecting Valium tablets, returning to his birthplace, and deceiving others about his intentions by appearing more sociable and optimistic. He stopped gambling. In sessions he talked about his earlier suicide attempts as well as his mother's attempt on her life.

At this critical point in the analysis, the analyst saw himself, in retrospect, as a guard going to sleep at his post. In this case, the decisive factor in precipitating the suicide attempt was the relaxation, encouraged by the patient, of vigilance regarding the suicide risk, a lessening of empathic contact with the patient, and an enactment of his father's withdrawal and failure to stake a claim for his child's right to a relationship with him by not protecting Mr Adams's analytic time and place with the analyst.

Later, in his analysis, it became clear that fantasies enacted in his gambling had been displaced on to his suicide fantasy including the belief that he would omnipotently triumph over the loss of his father and be chosen by fate/mother. The pre-suicide stage, like gambling, is a manic flight from judgement into narcissism.

Mr Adams was unconsciously in the grip of a repetition compulsion and had tested the analyst to see if he would repeat his earlier experience with his father. The analyst's response to Mr Adams' behaviour (e.g. an apparent improvement and the undetected meaning of a narcissistic withdrawal) coincided with his breaking of the analytic structure (by cancelling sessions) that he failed to prevent. This failure was experienced by the patient as a failure to maintain the reality of the analytic relationship, that is, the realities of time and place, thereby leaving the patient without an alternative to the timeless merging fantasy of his suicide scenario. Mr Adams left the analyst to return to his mother. The analyst failed to recognise the merging fantasy that was gratified in this way and the destructiveness inherent in it.

This empathic failure was experienced by Mr Adams as an enactment in the transference of the neglectful pre-Oedipal father who sanctioned his youngest son's return to a seductive and 'murderous' mother. In this way, the analyst unwittingly entered into and played a role in the patient's suicide fantasy.

Just prior to attempting suicide Mr Adams cancelled his sessions. At the same time, the analyst underestimated the imminence of the suicidal act. There is no explicit or implicit suggestion that these two features occur only with suicidal patients, but these features may have particular meaning during a pre-suicide state.

The analysis of a pre-suicide state based on material from before and after Mr Adams' suicide attempt illuminated the father transference, which had been enacted in the analyst's countertransference and the cancelled sessions. The transference was to a father who failed to claim his child for himself, who abandoned him to a smothering, 'murderous' mother, and who did not offer an alternative to an exclusive mother/child fusion. The father had not stood in the way of a regressive pull to a sadomasochistic relationship with mother, which formed the core of the suicide fantasy. The patient, who, in turn, left the analyst to join his mother in death, reversed his experience of being abandoned by his father.

The analyst is involved simultaneously in two basic transferential experiences: first, the repetition of a dyadic primitive struggle with a mother who will murder by smothering her child or abandoning it to starve; and, second, as the father who fails to rescue the child from the pathological maternal relationship by intervening and offering an alternative object. The patient is likely to draw the analyst into recognising only one transference at the expense of the other.

Note

1   The following views were first developed in Campbell (1995).

References

Abelin, E. (1978). The role of the father in the pre-Oedipal years. *Journal of the American Psycoanalytic Association, 26*, 143–161.

Campbell, D. (1995). The role of the father in a pre-suicide state. *International Journal of Psychoanalysis, 76*, 315–323.

Freud, S. (1931). Female sexuality. In J. Strachey (Ed.), *The standard edition of the complete psychological works of Sigmund Freud (Vol. 21)*. London: Hogarth Press

Greenson, R (1968). Dis-identifying from mother. *International Journal of Psycho-Analysis, (49)*, 370–374.

Loewald, H. W. (1951). Ego and reality. *International Journal of Psycho-Analysis, 32*, 10–18.

Mahler, M. S. & Gosliner, B. J. (1955). On symbiotic child psychosis—genetic, dynamic and restitutive aspects. *Psychoanalytic Study of the Child, 10*, 195–212.

Chapter 8

Pre-suicide states in adolescence

The impact of puberty and adolescent development

Professionals working with suicidal adolescents are aware that their anxieties about the safety of their patients are not misplaced. Suicide among young people is a major mental health issue in the United Kingdom. 'Suicide accounts for 20 percent of all deaths amongst young people aged 15–24 and is the second most common cause of death amongst young people after accidental death. Around 19,000 young people attempt suicide every year and about 700 of these die as a result. Young women aged between 15 and 19 years are the group most likely to attempt suicide; however, young men are much more likely to die as a result of their suicide attempt. Latest figures show the peak difference, both in terms of the number of suicides and rate, is in the 20–24 age group, where there are five male suicides for each female suicide' (Department of Health, 2014, p. 6). While suicide has been more prevalent among adolescents and young people between the ages of 15 and 24, research in the USA in the 1990's indicated an alarming trend of escalating suicide rates among 5 to 14 year olds (Pfeffer, 1990). In the UK, suicide verdicts are not returned for children under 10 years of age. However, there are some indicators that this trend is emerging in the UK. There were six deaths for children aged 10–14 in 2012, a decrease from nine in 2011 (Department of Health, 2014). A report by the National Society for Prevention of Cruelty to Children (Harker, Jutte, Murphy, Bentley, Miller & Fitch, 2013) suggests that this decrease in fatalities may be due to an increase in counselling sessions where suicidal feelings or self-harm were the main concern for the third year running.

The idiosyncratic and multi-determined nature of suicidal acts and the complexity of adolescent development compel those working with suicidal adolescents to develop further their theory and clinical technique. It is not surprising that psychoanalysts have been exploring the subject of suicide in adolescence since the early years of psychoanalysis.

As we mentioned earlier, the Vienna Psychoanalytic Society held a symposium in 1910 entitled *On Suicide: With Particular Reference to Suicide Among Young Students*. Wilhelm Stekel's (1910) contribution to the symposium identified revenge as a motivating factor in the suicide act. 'I am inclined to feel that the principle of Talion plays the decisive role here. No one kills himself who has never wanted to kill another or at least wished the death of another.' He went on to explore the nature of the relationship between the suicidal young person and his or her parent: 'The child wants to rob his parents of their greatest and most precious possession, his own life. The child knows that thereby he will inflict the greatest pain. Thus, the punishment the child imposes upon himself is simultaneously punishment he imposes on the instigators of his sufferings' (pp. 87–89).

Two features of adolescence, which we will explore further in this chapter, make adolescents particularly vulnerable to suicide and often arouse grave concern in those who are working with suicidal adolescents: 1) the consequences of physical and hormonal changes initiated by puberty, and 2) the labile nature of impulses and defences during adolescence. The first characteristic forces the adolescent's body to the centre of the psychic stage as a source of excitement, fascination and curiosity. There is a preoccupation with the developing sexually potent and aggressive body as it is integrated into the adolescent's self-image and relationships. The same body may also be a source of confusion and anxiety. Pubertal changes revive earlier repressed Oedipal fantasies that put a strain on the adolescent's defences.

Just a brief word about how we think about the Oedipus complex. We have observed in young children a complex set of fantasies and feelings about their parents (real and/or imagined) that Freud identified as echoing the dynamics of the Greek myth of Oedipus. There are differences of opinion among psychoanalysts about the timing of the Oedipal phase. Originally, the Oedipal phase was thought to occur usually from about three and half years to about six. Kleinian analysts believe that the Oedipal phase begins much earlier. However, for the purposes of our subject we are not concerned with the timing, but with the nature of the Oedipus complex itself. The complex feelings, which make up the Oedipal phase of development, include sexual rivalry with the parent of the same sex, usually, and fantasies about birth and pregnancy. The successful negotiation of the Oedipal complex 'results in the creation of the incest barrier, acceptance of generational boundaries, entry into the temporal dimension of life, respect for the value of waiting and effort, and formation of the superego' (Akhtar, 2009). When a child is unable for whatever reason to navigate their way through the Oedipal phase they may be vulnerable to developing neurotic conflicts and symptoms or having a breakdown. These original Oedipal feelings and fantasies are revived again with the onset of puberty to be worked through in the context of a new, adult sexual body.

The second characteristic of adolescence is a fluidity and flexibility that gives this phase of development an inherent instability. Risk, experimentation and unpredictability are necessary for further development. Normal progress is often made by two-steps-forward-one-step backward. However, some adolescents may not be able to move forward and, instead, regress to infantile defences and concrete thinking to defend against unbearable states of confusion or anxiety. A suicidal thought and/or action arising from a regressed state is not only confusing and shaming, but is also gratifying, and as such, represents a compromise formation as Biven and Daldin (2005, p. 41) have drawn our attention to.

When paranoid and concrete thinking accompany reliance upon projective mechanisms, the body may become the object of projections and paranoid delusions. Adolescence is also a time of action as the adolescent experiments with new behaviour and exercises omnipotent fantasies. When the adolescent's body is experienced as the source of maddening thoughts and feelings, it may become the target of an active attack in the form of cutting and suicide, or more covert suicide in anorexia nervosa. It is the conjunction of primitive defences and proneness to act in the already volatile adolescent that significantly increases the risk of acts of suicide and self-destruction during this phase of development.

The impact of puberty on the body image

The first substantial contribution to psychoanalytic thinking on the subject of adolescence appeared in 1905 when Freud (1905) published *Three Essays on the Theory of Sexuality*. In Chapter III, 'The Transformations of Puberty', Freud identified three changes activated by the onset of puberty: 1) the emergence of the genitals as the dominant erotogenic zone over the earlier oral and anal component instincts, 2) a shift from a predominately auto-erotic sexual orientation to the finding of a sexual object, and 3) the consolidation of passive and active, masculine and feminine character traits from inherent bisexuality. Although Freud was not the first to recognise the existence of bi-sexuality in human beings, he made behavioural, constitutional and psychological bi-sexuality one of the cornerstones of his theory of sexuality. In this way Freud laid the groundwork for psychoanalytic understanding of the relationship between puberty, adolescence, psychopathology and adult sexuality. We are impressed by the way parents of both sexes are objects of identification and desire, to the extent that masculine and feminine attitudes and homosexual and heterosexual erotic tendencies exist in all individuals. The adolescent's response to and resolution of the conflicts engendered by these three changes determine the character of the final sexual organisation. We are also aware that some adolescents feel confused and ashamed of their infantile sexual impulses, masturbatory habits and fantasies and bi-sexuality to the extent that they disown or attack their sexual bodies. These adolescents are often at risk of suicide.

The female body image

Before puberty the little girl has had to struggle with the upsetting reality that she cannot compete with mother by bearing a child of her own. Usually the girl copes with this narcissistic wound by accepting the reality of sexual and generational differences (Chasseguet-Smirgal, 1985), and holding on to an image of a maternal and heterosexual mother with which to identify more fully during and after puberty when her uterus develops the capacity to sustain life, and her clitoris and vagina can be used comfortably in sexual intercourse (Laufer & Laufer, 1989).

With the advent of puberty, Oedipal and pre-Oedipal attractions and rivalries are revived with fundamental differences: the musculature and the reproductive organs complete their development so that girls have the capacity to bear their father's child and carry out death wishes towards mother. As a consequence of the sexual maturing of her body and influenced by the incest taboo, the adolescent girl is faced with two primary tasks: taking over care and protection of her body from her parents, and developing heterosexual relationships with non-incestuous objects.

Puberty also revives the concept of the internalised Oedipal father along with the internalised pre-Oedipal father. The adolescent girl's experience of having a place in the pre-Oedipal father's mind, which offered consolation for his loss as a sexual partner during the dissolution of the Oedipus complex and motivated acceptance of the Oedipal father as representative of the incest barrier, can be revived during adolescence to provide internal support when earlier conflicts are reworked.

However, persistent anxiety about abandonment or engulfment by mother may arouse irreconcilable hostility towards the mother and lead the adolescent girl to attack the mother's sadistic feeding behaviour by taking over the feeding function, controlling intake, or actively rejecting food by refusing to eat or vomiting what has been taken in. A split-off part of the child identifies with the aggressor, the mother, who they feel has abandoned them to die or intrusively dominated them with inappropriate feeds. In this unconscious state of mind the body, representing a bad, greedy child-self, is attacked. The most severe cases of eating disorders, like anorexia nervosa and bulimia, are covertly suicidal.

In another scenario, desperate attempts to get close to an unavailable mother may arouse unacceptable homosexual anxieties in the girl and lead her to abandon a feminine image of her body as too close to the threatening mother. When the girl's search for a substitute mother in the father or a triumphant Oedipal attachment is frustrated by father's absence or unavailability, the pubertal girl may seek safety and compensation by identifying her body with father's. If this identification with father's body persists beyond puberty, the adolescent girl may believe that her unfeminine body is incapable of producing a child. Becoming pregnant may be felt to be the only means of filling the emptiness left by the estrangement from mother and overcoming the fear of having an unfeminine body (Laufer & Laufer, 1984). When pregnancy is not an option or it fails as a solution, the adolescent girl may actively attack her body by self-mutilation, or try to get rid of her unfeminine body altogether when suicide becomes a viable solution.

The male body image

Before puberty the little boy has had to come to terms with the fact that he cannot compete with father's potent penis and physical strength in the battle for mother's sexual attention. During latency, the boy, like the girl, copes with the realization that Oedipal wishes cannot be gratified and accepts sexual and generational differences. However, the boy attempts to preserve a positive image of a potent and heterosexual father with which to identify more fully during and after puberty, when his genitals develop the capacity to impregnate women.

With the onset of puberty Oedipal and pre-Oedipal attractions and rivalries are revived with the same fundamental differences that affect girls: the musculature and the reproductive organs complete their development so that boys have the capacity to impregnate mother and carry out death wishes towards father. As a consequence of the sexual maturing of his body and influenced by the incest taboo, the adolescent boy, like the girl, is faced with two primary tasks: taking over care and protection of his body from his parents, and developing heterosexual relationships with non-incestuous objects.

Puberty also revives the internalised Oedipal father along with the internalised pre-Oedipal father. The adolescent boy's experience of having a place in the pre-Oedipal father's mind is consolation for his loss of mother as a sexual partner during the dissolution of the Oedipus complex. A positive attachment to and co-identification with father as well as peers supports and motivates acceptance of the Oedipal rival as representative of the incest barrier, which can be revived during adolescence to provide internal support when earlier conflicts are reworked.

The immediate consequence of a failed or pathological attachment to father before puberty for both boys and girls is an increase in dependency and attachment to mother in the child's search for security and nurture. If the mother does not have a positive paternal imago with which the boy can identify, or relates to her son narcissistically in order to meet her own needs, the boy is likely to share with the girl similar pre-Oedipal Core Complex fears about engulfment and abandonment. The persistence of pre-genital anxieties may make genitally oriented heterosexual Oedipal fantasies too dangerous to entertain, and may undermine the boy's efforts to find a suitable masculine object with which to identify in order to separate from his mother and claim his body as his own. Conflicts arising out of a failure to negotiate an Oedipal phase of development will be revived in puberty and may lead to a rejection of an active, phallic body image, and contemplation of homosexuality or suicide.

Homosexuality in adolescence

Shame and guilt in reaction to homosexual fantasies and activity during adolescence may contribute to some young people contemplating suicide, that is, killing a body which is perceived as abnormal or perverse. However, homosexuality in adolescence is frequently misunderstood by adolescents and adults, and by laymen and professionals. We believe that pejorative associations and judgmental views about homosexuality are unacceptable and undermine attempts to understand the nature and function of homosexuality in an adolescent.

Psychoanalysis has been criticised for seeing homosexuality as a perversion in the same way fetishism, paedophilia, etc. Freud (1920) distinguished between homosexuality and other sexual aberrations, arguing that homosexuals who come into treatment are not representative of the whole group; many homosexuals are not ill, cannot be 'cured', and can relate to others as whole objects, and there is a capacity for love, concern and sublimation.

Homosexuality is not a single, uniform phenomenon. We feel it is more accurate to think about homosexualities, just as we would think about heterosexualities, in a developmental context, as we explained earlier. Although the first attachment for both boys and girls is the mother, or the person who provides the earliest maternal care, children of both sexes attach themselves to parent of the opposite sex. In boys this love of the father is accompanied by the wish to replace the mother and have the father as a permanent partner. During this phase the mother is seen as a rival for the father. Psychoanalysts characterise this developmental period as the negative Oedipal phase to differentiate it from a later phase, referred to as the positive Oedipal phase, when the boy wishes to have his mother as his sexual partner and get rid of his rival, the father. Some boys and, later, men report that the crush on their father never subsided, that they never wanted to leave their father, that they never 'fell in love' with their mother. For these boys the negative Oedipal phase was never conflictual, or transitional, but was the permanent expression of their sexual longing. These boys report that the conflicts that ensued arose not from their choice of father and, later, other men as sexual objects, but from the social and cultural ostracism, hostility and sometimes violent persecution.

Different types of homosexuality may emerge during early, middle and late adolescence. Homosexuality serves many functions and is not necessarily a final solution when it is pursued in early adolescence. Mervin Glasser (1977) observed that homosexual activity during the early phase of adolescence often relies upon idealisation and feminine identifications for primarily narcissistic gratification. Glasser identifies an identificatory facility to live a role, which is prominent in adolescence and is utilised to defend against the painful reality of differences between self and object. Co-identification and the formation of passionate and erotic bonds with other males is often a rehearsal for later heterosexual performance. Although sexual activity is with a contemporary male, the fantasies are heterosexual. These early defensive identificatory mechanisms are usually outgrown by late adolescence. While homosexual behaviour in early adolescence may function to protect the young adolescent from his or her strong regressive wishes, homosexuality in middle adolescence reflects the presence of inhibiting castration anxieties leading to crippling fears of the opposite sex and the adoption of a passive submissive attitude towards rivals of the same sex. Late adolescence is a time of integration and consolidation, and homosexuality, at this time, is unlikely to change. We have focused on homosexual development in boys. Although there are some parallels in the development of homosexual development in girls, there are some significant differences. For instance, the use of masturbation to gratify sexual fantasies may be more problematic if the girl identifies her own hand with the mother's soothing hand, thereby intensifying the regressive longing for the mother (Laufer, M.E., 1982).

Identification with the aggressor, asceticism, altruism and intellectualization

It is worth noting four defences, identified by Anna Freud (1936), which are prominent during adolescence: identification with the aggressor, asceticism, altruism and intellectualisation. Although identification with the aggressor is apparent in very young children, it re-emerges in adolescence when young people seek to defend against a dangerous sexual or aggressive individual by becoming the threatening object through identification or impersonation. The adolescent then projects threatening aggressive and sexual aspects back into the external world. As we said earlier, no person attempts to kill himself or herself who has not, in some way, felt that one or both parent rejected their body or wished him or her dead. Federn (1929) expressed it thus: 'No one kills themselves who has not been wished dead by another.' This experience is repeated in the provocation of neglect or rejection, which projects guilt associated with self-destructive impulses and is experienced by the adolescent as a sanction of the suicidal act.

There is a labile quality in adolescence that makes it difficult to contain ideas and feelings without resorting to action. Consequently, thoughts and fantasies are often experienced as dangerous because of the fear that they will break out in behaviour. Defences such as asceticism, altruism and intellectualisation, unlike identification with the aggressor, are mobilised to stop action. Asceticism, the practice of self-denial and abstention from worldly comforts and pleasures, is a defence that attempts to avoid persecution by a superego that is critical of sexuality activity. Or, asceticism may be accompanied by altruism, if the adolescent projects forbidden sexual or aggressive wishes onto another, identifies with the other, and assists the other in fulfilling their sexual wishes. In this way, the adolescent is able, via identification, to obtain gratification vicariously.

However, even when the individual does not respond to the upsurge of sexual and aggressive impulses at puberty by acting on them, those impulses may generate feelings of shame, guilt or loss of control and identity, and prompt the adolescent to channel these unacceptable impulses into intellectualisation, such as engaging in rumination or endless intellectual discussions on abstract, political and philosophical themes.

Masturbation in adolescence

During a pre-suicide state, the perpetrator's body, identified with unacceptable thoughts, feelings and actions, is the object of a lethal attack. As we have explained, the advent of puberty thrusts the adolescent's body onto the centre of his or her psychic stage. Laufer and Laufer (1989) believed that the adolescent's capacity to integrate their genitality into their self-image depended upon the young man or woman's capacity to shift from their original view of their genitals as passive in relation to the object to believing that their genitals could be an active component in relationships. Masturbation, especially for boys, is a primary medium through which the adolescent may resolve passive and active conflicts in relation to their genitals. The outcome of these conflicts is a major factor in shaping the adolescent's overall sexual body image.

Moe Laufer (1976) viewed masturbation for the male adolescent as 'equivalent to trial action', that is, as an auto-erotic activity which helps to integrate regressive fantasies as part of the effort to achieve genital dominance. It is critical that trial action by masturbation has an active quality so that the adolescent feels he is in charge of his body and can actively test (consciously and unconsciously) his central masturbation fantasy to determine 'which sexual thoughts, feelings, or gratifications are acceptable to the superego, and which of these are unacceptable and therefore must not be allowed to participate in the establishment of the final sexual organisation' (p. 302). Pathology develops when pre-genital fantasies and gratifications dominate genital ones, in some cases leaving the adolescent helpless in relation to shameful fantasies and passive in relation to his sexual body.

Egle Laufer (1982) argues that the adolescent girl responds differently to the prospect of masturbation than is the case with boys. The conflict over masturbation for the girl arises not in the content of the masturbation fantasy, but on the activity of the hand, which permits the adolescent to experience the body as a source of satisfaction independent of the mother. The revival of Oedipal wishes in the sexually mature adolescent girl creates a homosexual conflict with the girl's need to identify her body with her mother's body; a body that is viewed ambivalently as reproductive and nurturing, on the one hand, and hated and depriving, on the other hand.

Today it is commonly accepted that adolescence begins with the advent of puberty. However, it is more difficult to identify the end of adolescence. We think of adolescence coming to an end when the individual's sexual organisation becomes fixed and does not change without therapeutic intervention. This is not to say that the end of adolescence necessarily resolves the three tasks of adolescence outlined above. But it does mean that unresolved conflicts remain so and options for changing established patterns of relating and ways of thinking and acting are radically decreased.

References

Akhtar, S. (2009). *Comprehensive dictionary of psychoanalysis.* London: Karnac.

Biven, B. (1993) with Daldin, H. Suicide in adolescence as a compromise formation. *Psychoanalytic Social Work, 4,* 23–49. And (2005) In *True pretences.* Leicester: Matador. pp. 26–42.

Chasseguet-Smirgal, J. (1985). *The ego ideal.* London: Free Association Books.

Department of Health. (2014). *Statistical update on suicide.* London: HM Government.

Federn, P. (1929). Selbstmordprophylaxe in der Analyse. *Verlag der Zeitschrift für Psychoanalytische Pädagogik, 3,* 379–389.

Freud, S. (1905). Three essays on the theory of sexuality. In J. Strachey (Ed. and Trans.), *The standard edition of the complete psychological works of Sigmund Freud (Vol. 7).* London: Hogarth Press.

Freud, S. (1920). The psychogenesis of a case of homosexuality in a woman. In J. Strachey (Ed.), *The standard edition of the complete psychological works of Sigmund Freud (Vol. 18),* pp. 146–173. London: Hogarth Press.

Freud, A. (1936, revised 1966). *The ego and the mechanisms of defence.* New York: International University Press.

Glasser, M. (1977). Homosexuality in adolescence. *British Journal of Medical Psychology, 50*(3), 217–225. doi: 10.1111/j.2044-8341.1977.tb02417.x

Harker, L., Jutte, S., Murphy, T., Bentley, H., Miller, P. & Fitch, K. (2013). *How safe are our children.* NSPCC.

Laufer, M. (1976). The central masturbation fantasy, the final sexual organization, and adolescence. *Psychoanalytic Study of the Child, 31,* 297–316.

Laufer, M. E. (1982). Female masturbation in adolescence and the development of the relationship to the body. *International Journal of Psycho-Analysis, 63*, 295–302.

Laufer, M. & Laufer, M. E. (1984). *Adolescence and developmental breakdown: A psychoanalytic view*. New Haven, CT US: Yale University Press.

Laufer, M. & Laufer, M. E. (1989). *Developmental breakdown and psychoanalytic treatment in adolescence: Clinical studies*. New Haven, CT US: Yale University Press.

Office for National Statistics. (2014). *Suicides in the United Kingdom*, 2012 Registrations. ONS: London.

Pfeffer, C. R. (1990). Suicidal behavior in children and adolescents: a clinical and research perspective. *Yale Journal of Biology and Medicine, Jul–Aug, 63*(4), 325–332.

Stekel, W. (1910). Symposium on suicide. *On suicide* (pp. 33–141). New York: International Universities Press.

Chapter 9

Implications for the professional

The principal danger for the professional working with suicidal clients lies in minimising the pre-suicidal state or missing it altogether. The dicing-with-death syndrome is built upon minimising the risk of failure and heightening the excitement at the prospect of triumph. The therapist may get caught up in the excitement of a gamble or of watching his patient 'have a go', and fail to see the more hidden excitement in the revengeful use of failure. On the other hand, in over-reacting to anxiety and taking responsibility for the patient's body, the therapist may gratify in the transference the patient's wish to shift the responsibility for his body from himself to the analyst, and, as we describe on page 55, make the analyst the executioner (Asch, 1980). The therapist's active intervention to prohibit risk-taking may also reinforce the patient's passivity and, as a consequence, raise his anxiety.

The combination of fantasies which emerges during the pre-suicide state is fulfilled by the suicidal act. Therefore, we believe it is critical during the pre-suicide state for the professional to give priority to understanding the suicide fantasies and to conveying this understanding to their client as the principal way of defusing the client's need to act out their suicide fantasies. It is also important not to become caught in the patient's unconscious traps that he or she will inevitably set. Since we also feel this task is easier to write about than it is to achieve in practice, we offer ten danger signals (some of which will be familiar), which could alert the professional to the existence of a pre-suicide state.

Ten danger signals

The case of Mr Adams (see Chapters 6 and 7) will serve to illustrate many of the danger signals, which can be recognised during the pre-suicide state. These fall into three categories: the historical, those identifiable in the patient's current life situation, and those occurring within the transference with the analyst.

The historical

1) A previous suicide attempt.

Mr Adams made a suicide attempt about three years earlier. Those who have attempted suicide once represent a 27-fold greater risk of subsequent successful suicide compared with the general population (Hawton & Fagg, 1988). There are several tasks facing someone who is motivated to work through their attempt to kill him or herself: 1) becoming aware of his or her original suicide fantasy, 2) taking responsibility for the suicidal act in order to work through the guilt associated with having abandoned the body to a homicidal ego, and 3) mourning the assault on their body. Finally, there is the task of resolving the conflicts that were dealt with by an attempt to kill the body. Unless this last task is completed, the body will still be at risk to another lethal attack and suicide will remain a secret weapon, a trump card which may be played whenever the original conflicts re-emerge.

2) A propensity to deal with internal conflict via action.

Mr Adams played the horses whenever he became depressed. He sought to be the favourite son of fate. It was fate, not Mr Adams, which resolved problems. The patient who habitually deals with internal conflicts via external action will be more vulnerable to acting on a suicidal impulse when he is unable to make use of the activity that provides relief. In this case, Mr Adams had gambled away all of his money – half a million pounds. Loan sharks were pressuring him.

3) An actual or attempted suicide by a parent or a close relative.

Two months before Mr Adams' suicide attempt, his mother had tried to kill herself by taking a massive overdose. Actual or attempted suicide by a parent or close relative may well precipitate a suicide attempt by a spouse, son or daughter. In Mr Adams' case, his mother's unsuccessful attempt on her life increased his guilt because he had ignored her explicit warnings that she would kill herself. His fear of her increased as well. He made a significant verbal slip when telling his analyst of his mother's suicide attempt: 'My mother tried to kill myself'. This was the mother/ killer with which his body was identified.

The current life situation

4) A recently experienced failure, particularly of a sexual relationship.

Mr Adams had recently lost several important clients. Many suicidal patients suffer from poor self-esteem, are severely self-critical and feel themselves to be failures. An actual failure, for example getting sacked or failing an examination, is a danger signal because it is experienced as confirmation by the outside world of what the patient feels about himself.

Hope for rescue from outside is lost. The persecutory self has irrefutable evidence from outside of inner badness or worthlessness.

5) A withdrawal from others into the body.

When Mr Adams arrived for his first session, he was dishevelled, unshaven, withdrawn and lethargic. Mr Adams' withdrawal from others and neglect of his body point to a shift from acting out conflicts with others, to acting them out with his body.

6) An attempt to blackmail with suicide.

Judging from Mr Adams' wife's response, it appears that there was at least an explicit suggestion of suicide to blackmail her into rescuing him. This is a danger signal familiar to all those working with or living with suicidal patients, but one that may not be taken seriously enough. A professional may well react negatively to the sadistic and manipulative aspects of the blackmail and dismiss the patient, as did Mr Adams' wife, with near fatal results.

In fact, it is difficult for analysts and relatives to avoid being placed in a double bind. Threats of blackmail may arise before a holiday break, when the patient has to separate from his analyst and cope without his support. Paraphrasing Asch (1980), implicit or explicit blackmail has this message: 'Unless you see me more often or cancel your holiday, I will kill myself. I will commit suicide because you failed me. It will be your fault. You will have driven me to it. You will have killed me'. The danger in giving in to this demand is that it will endorse the fantasy that someone else can completely take over responsibility for the patient's body, and in so doing sanction the abdication of responsibility for his actions. The worker will have to find ways of making this aspect of the fantasy clear to the patient, especially his wish to deny his own violence towards his body and the sadistic use of it against others.

On the other hand, the suicidal individual may experience the practitioner's refusal to satisfy these demands as a rejection, as though abandoning them to die. This is why blackmail must always be taken seriously. Beneath the sadomasochistic dynamic may lay a terror that the patient no longer feels safe in his own hands and is really asking for protection against himself.

7) Consent or collusion between the patient and others in a suicidal fantasy.

An experience of rejection or a feeling of having been abandoned or dismissed, especially when it comes from someone who is valued, may be the precipitating factor in the actual attack on the body during the pre-suicidal state. It was after his wife refused to come to him, and, in effect, told him to get on with his plan to kill himself, that Mr Adams took an overdose. As previously mentioned, Straker (1958) points out, 'A decisive factor in a successful suicide attempt appears to be the implied consent or unconscious collusion between the patient and the person most involved in the psychic struggle' (p. 479).

Those working with suicidal individuals are vulnerable to being provoked or subtly led into attitudes and reactions, which are experienced by the individual as rejection or collusion in the suicidal fantasy. This is what happened when the analyst failed to prevent Mr Adams from cancelling his sessions in order to go to Edinburgh where he planned to kill himself. He wanted the analyst to see that attending his sessions was a matter of life and death because behind his business plan was a suicide plan. During his therapy there had been signs of improvement in his appearance, attitude and life outside the session. Therapeutic work had focused on such danger signals as his gambling, his earlier suicide attempt and his mother's attempt on her life. The analyst's mistake was that he let him go. Why?

It later became apparent that in Mr Adams' therapy the analyst had failed to recognise a shift in the balance of power between two suicide fantasies, with near fatal consequences. After his mother's attempt on her life, which he experienced as an attack on his life, Mr Adams developed an assassination fantasy. The aim of this first suicide fantasy was to escape the assassin-mother by identifying her with his body and then killing that body. The analyst was alerted to the existence of the assassination fantasy by its enactment in Mr Adams' neglect of his body, slovenly dress and poor hygiene. In this way, the analyst was able to bring Mr Adams' assassination fantasy into the analysis.

However, a second suicide fantasy that Mr Adams could merge with an idealised, asexual, omnipotently gratifying mother became a delusional conviction. Unfortunately, there was no challenge to this delusion because his father failed to intervene and did not offer an alternative object with whom Mr Adams could identify. Mr Adams believed that this fantasy of merging with his mother, which developed out of the first assassination fantasy, could be actualised once the assassin-mother, now identified with his body, had been killed. This belief motivated Mr Adams to plan his suicide. He became calm and optimistic because he now had a secret solution to his conflicts. The merging fantasy escaped detection because it was accompanied by apparent improvement.

8) The formation of a suicide plan.

The wish to die and the accompanying suicide fantasy may wax and wane in the patient's consciousness. The formation of a suicide plan, that is the scheme for carrying out the suicide fantasy, heralds the acute pre-suicide state. The suicide fantasy may include a method of killing the body, but the development of a suicide plan includes the details of time and place. Pills, a weapon or equipment may be collected. The attention to detail will vary, but any evidence of a plan should be taken seriously.

However, secrecy is nearly always an important ingredient, and evidence of a suicide plan may be hard to discern. Attention to the patient's state of mind or feelings about himself may provide an important clue. There is frequently a kind of inner peace and a sense of control that accompanies the formation of a suicide plan. Any sudden change in the patient's affective state towards a relaxation or calm, rather than necessarily being an indication of improvement, should alert the practitioner that the patient may have formulated a suicide plan. From a technical point of view, the worker should try to elicit the details of the plan and bring it into the open. These details will illuminate the suicide fantasy.

In Mr Adams' case, his depression lifted as he implemented the details of his suicide plan. He collected Valium tablets, returned to his birthplace and deceived others about his intentions by appearing more sociable and optimistic. He was, in fact, in the midst of a narcissistic regression sustained by the prospect of imminently fulfilling his merging suicide fantasy. As far as the patient is concerned, he is already at peace because he has crossed a rational barrier of self-preservation and now positively identifies the assassin (his body) and has no doubt about killing it. In a sense, a psychic homicide has already occurred.

Case study: The uncle and the rock

This critical stage in the pre-suicidal state was described by a 15-year-old boy who was with his uncle over the weekend before the uncle killed himself on the following Thursday. 'It was as though Uncle George was already dead on Sunday. He had tied his life to a rock with a piece of string. He threw his life out of the window on Sunday but the rock didn't hit the ground until Thursday'.

Within the transference

9) The loss of concern both by the suicidal individual for him or herself, for others, and by others for him or her.

Emil Gutheil (1948; 1999) observed how suicidal individuals give up on themselves and die. He understood these individuals to be suffering from a withdrawal of narcissistic cathexis by a rejecting superego. Giving up on oneself leads to a withdrawal from life. One of the consequences of the suicidal individual's withdrawal from other people during a pre-suicidal phase, albeit behind a deceptive facade of sociability, is that the depressive affects, anxieties and fears are no longer communicated. As a result, those around the suicidal person may cease to respond to his needs and feelings as they ordinarily might do. Even if they have some intellectual awareness of the suicidal risk at this critical moment, the patient's narcissistic withdrawal cuts others off from any normal stimulus for empathic responses of alarm or concern (Tahka, 1978).

A suicide attempt may now be imminent because the patient is emotionally cut off from his friends, relatives or professional helpers who would ordinarily protect him from himself. The signal for this danger is the sudden loss of subjective emotional concern for a depressed or suicidal patient by those most involved with him. For the professional, the loss of concern may manifest itself as a failure to recognise the importance of the therapeutic relationship in the patient's life. In the case of Mr Adams the analyst was not able to maintain the centrality and reliability of the therapy. Mr Adams cancelled his sessions prior to the suicide attempts. It behoves the therapist of the suicidal patient to carefully scrutinise any impulse to relax his interpretive stance or disrupt the consistency of the therapeutic structure unless, of course, hospitalisation is required.

10) The appearance of countertransference reactions that may contribute to a loss of empathy or failure to perceive a psychic homicide.

This may manifest itself in many different ways. The suicidal patient's attempt to blackmail the analyst or provoke the analyst's collusion in a suicide plan may trigger countertransference reactions in the therapist that present a danger if they are not recognised and understood. In fact, any of the danger signals are likely to be manifest directly or symbolically in the transference. In Mr Adams' case, the analyst reacted to his narcissistic withdrawal by letting him temporarily leave his therapy and go to Edinburgh. Mr Adams then perceived the analyst as sanctioning and colluding with his suicide plan. The analyst's reaction, like that of Mr Adams' wife, was an essential ingredient in the fulfilment of the suicide plan. A further example will be given later.

A greater understanding of the danger signals may enable the therapist to play a more constructive role during a pre-suicide state. The danger is that if the signals are missed, the therapist may behave unwittingly like the patient's hostile internal object from the past that the patient can only overcome through death.

Management of a suicide attempt

It is hard to underestimate the value of the proper management of a suicide attempt. Even if the patient survives, it is a situation that offers the possibility of his either returning to the same vicious circle whence he came, or of helping him to move forward to something new. Whether or not the patient ends up in formal psychotherapy, the dynamics of this management bear careful study.

Attempted suicide is often seen as a crisis in the person's life, appropriately so if one considers the origin of the word crisis as both a threat but also a crossroads – an opportunity for change. Many people who have attempted suicide look back on it as a life defining moment. This is well described in A. Alvarez's (1974) study of his own suicide attempt *The Savage God.*

Many suicide attempts go undetected. The patient merely 'sleeps it off'. Sometimes relatives will allow this to happen. Their indifference may betoken their underlying animosity to the patient. When a general practitioner is called, even he too may decide that nothing needs to be done.

For the most part, however, the patient is referred to a busy casualty department where, with the exception of violent alcoholics, attempted suicides are among the least popular patients with both nursing and medical staff. This isn't helped by the fact that the patient is likely to be in a belligerent or aggressive state of mind, partly out of embarrassment. The result is that medical procedures, some of which are of very doubtful value, can be accompanied by such comments as, 'Why didn't you do it properly?' or 'Don't you think we've got better things to do with our time?' It is easy to condemn these attitudes, but in reality they represent a natural response to the patient's aggressive act. Some regard medical procedures, particularly stomach washout, as a potential deterrent to future attempts, and they certainly are experienced by the patient as painful and humiliating, but it is doubtful if they function as a deterrent.

Case study: The stomach washout

A patient was reminded of a statement he had made when he took a previous overdose that he would not do it again because he could not stand a stomach washout. He was asked whether these thoughts went through his mind when taking the current overdose. His reply was that his intention had been that there would not be a washout this time. The stomach washout can be seen as an attempt by the staff to regain control of the patient's body, a control that the patient has taken from the medical profession in swallowing the tablets that, in most cases, the patient's doctor had prescribed.

Where there is a medical reason for the patient to be admitted, he is fortunate. Having attacked his body, to be allowed, forced even, to regress and to have bodily needs placed first, may well be exactly what he needs psychologically. The hospital can act as a relatively neutral container for all of the patient's projections. What the patient does not need is contempt or disdain from the professional staff, hard as this is to avoid. Thus, supporting the staff of the acute medical wards that are dealing with suicide is an important part of the psychiatrist's work. Unfortunately, many patients are discharged or encouraged to discharge themselves without any psychological assessment, even though this is recommended by the Department of Health in the NICE guidelines (2004).

Assessment following a suicidal act

The assessment of the patient should take place as soon as possible after the patient has regained consciousness, because, even at this early stage, it offers an opportunity to begin therapy. However, if the therapist can be included in the original chaos and receives the basic raw projections immediately after the suicidal person regains consciousness, the need to repeat the suicidal act may be reduced. Once the process of repression and denial has started, the patient is likely to recreate the familiar sadomasochistic relationship but now with the therapist as partner. The patient's internal prediction is that the therapist will cause this relationship, too, to fail and that suicide will again be the only solution. Delay in identifying and owning the power of the suicide fantasies allows old defences to be re-erected, with the psychiatrist as an accomplice.

The assessment itself should have the following aims:

1 To identify severe psychiatric illness in order to arrange appropriate treatment.
2 To let the patient know that his actions are taken seriously by the therapist, even if not by himself.
3 To establish the extent to which the patient can look inwards at the reasons for his actions. Surprisingly, this is often much easier for the patient in the disturbed state of mind immediately following a suicide attempt. A helpful technique to encourage this process is that of the action replay. In this, the patient is encouraged to give a detailed account of the events leading up to the day of the suicide, to the hour and then the actual minute. As the patient recalls the details, both he and the therapist are often given much more direct access to the affects and fantasies which motivated the act.
4 To encourage the patient to keep access to unconscious processes and the possibility of psychotherapy open by offering both tentative interpretations. If the latter turns out not to be the case, little has been lost.
5 To ensure that the patient is not returned to the same sadomasochistic relationship from which he came. It is far safer to hand the patient over to the care of a willing neutral relative or friend. It is essential to impress upon this person the seriousness of what has happened.

If no such suitable person can be found, it will be necessary to admit the patient to a psychiatric ward until such time as the therapist and patient feel it is safe to let him return to his partner, family, friend or to living on his own. The general principle, as always, must be that the supportive matrix is sufficient to contain the patient's pathology.

The central purpose, then, is to establish a preliminary hypothesis as to the reasons for the events and why the suicide attempt was necessary, implying to the patient that it was not a meaningless act. Sometimes the patient will be eager to minimise or dismiss the importance of the act, reassuring the interviewer (and themselves) that it was a passing state of mind and inviting them to collude with the statement that it will not occur again. The disastrous consequences of this escape from the painful psychic reality are described in Chapter 3 and in the example below. It may be that the patient acknowledges little of the significance of what has happened – this will come later; but a potentially dangerous situation will exist if the interviewer can give no real account of why things happened because s/he has then been drawn in to the patient's process of denial. The patient has wiped out the professional's capacity for independent thought.

Therapy should start as soon as possible. The appointment must be within a period of time that the patient can manage. It is crucial that the therapist stays alive in the patient's mind. In this acute phase, the promise of a session in two days may feel like never: that is, too long for the patient to hold the therapist in his thinking. A central belief of the suicidal person is that he has the capacity to kill off all of his good objects. To offer him an appointment beyond his own time span, or with a person whom he has not met, will be perceived as both a further rejection and confirmation of his belief in his own destructiveness.

The cornerstone of any treatment must be the reliability of the therapist.

As has been previously described (p. 23) the attachment pattern of many of those who carry out suicidal acts is dominated by anxiety, particularly separation anxiety. Perhaps the strongest empirical evidence comes from the study by Lukaschek and colleagues (2014) who set out to identify determinants of railway suicides in individuals receiving inpatient psychiatric treatment. They compared 101 suicide cases with a control group of 101 discharged patients matched for age, gender and diagnosis. Amongst the multiple factors that they studied, 'the most salient finding was the vital impact of a change of therapist . . . which resulted in a more than 20 fold increase in suicide risk in the final multivariate analysis'.

Some might see dependence as pathological, but we would see true independence as coming only from the experience of reliable and predictable dependence. Breaks in treatment can all too easily be experienced as rejection. Therefore, it is crucially important to anticipate such breaks and to emphasise to the patient (as well as the staff caring for them) the danger, which they may seek to deny. Many of the cases to which we have referred are illustrative but particularly the account given in Chapter 6.

Family therapy may be an appropriate mode of intervention when a pre-suicide state is identified in an adolescent or following an unsuccessful suicide attempt. Richman (1986), and Richman and Rosenbaum (1970; 1996) address the meaning of ambivalence, hostility and death wishes of significant others and their impact on suicidally vulnerable individuals.

The point in the cycle of suicide described above at which the professional enters the patient's world is of crucial importance. Often this is a matter of chance, determined by the duty rota, etc. However, there is often a delay of a few days between a suicidal attempt and the start of a proper psychotherapeutic engagement. Usually the therapist is involved after the patient has crossed the body barrier, enacted the suicidal fantasies, and, on this occasion, survived. It is our contention that, unless the therapist is closely involved with the initial suicidal breakdown, the patient may well be forced to re-enact the suicide attempt involving the therapist as an active (and often negligent or complicit) participant in a process in which the patient's life is put at risk. This represents a repetition of the dynamics that motivated the original suicide attempt. However, if the therapy goes well, the actions may be restricted to a suicide equivalent rather than an actual attempt.

At best the patient should be seen within 24–48 hours of the attempt and preferably in the hospital in which the medical consequences are being treated. If the patient has had the opportunity for more than one night's dream work, the primitive fantasies are likely to have been returned to the unconscious, where they will find nonverbal expression in the patient's subsequent behaviour. It is the therapist's job to keep these fantasies available to the patient, however painful this may be. The forces of denial and repression offer short-term respite but long-term danger.

Case study: An opportunity lost

A patient was seen, albeit too briefly, within 24 hours of a serious overdose. She said that she had been contemplating, but putting off, therapy for some time. The suicide attempt convinced her that she now needed therapy.

The interviewing psychiatrist reassessed her and gave her an appointment for a week later. She came to the outpatient appointment and said that she had been thinking things over. She had decided against entering therapy after all. The therapist reminded her of her exact words the previous week. She replied, 'That was a different person.' The opportunity had been lost.

The attempt had not been sufficiently explored and the wounds kept open. A temporary pathological healing had taken place. What subsequently happened to her is not known.

Case study: Deirdre – An opportunity not lost

The consequences of delay are clearer in the next example. It happened to one of the authors (Rob Hale) some twenty-five years ago, and it is perhaps only after retirement that it seems possible to admit to what happened. (Rob Hale uses the first person.)

Deirdre attempted suicide at the age of 18. She was the only child of extremely religious parents. As a child she had the experience of constant disapproval. She felt that her 'normal' naughtiness was seen by her parents as confirmation that she was not the child they wanted. She sought risks and pushed the boundaries. In adolescence, predictably, she took sexual risks and, perhaps inevitably, was raped by a stranger in a place where she should not have been. Predictably, she could not tell her parents, and her response was to become very promiscuous – effectively regaining the control she had lost in the rape (an example of identification with the aggressor).

Again predictably, she became pregnant and was unable to tell her parents. She came to London and had an abortion. She got a job and embarked on a series of brief relationships in which she would meet men once or twice then arrange a further meeting but would stand the man up. She would sit in her bedroom thinking with pleasure of the man waiting expectantly for her and then feeling confused, humiliated and rejected. Eventually, a man whom she was quite keen on turned the tables and did not turn up. Her response was to take a large overdose of analgesics. She was admitted to a medical ward.

I was on holiday so she was seen by a colleague and, after a brief spell on the psychiatric ward, she was referred to me for psychotherapy. I was struck by her composure and, although she recounted the events of her life quite clearly, she brought little of the affective quality into the room. The recent events were 'history', which could be kept in the past. I arranged to see her twice weekly. I noticed that I felt more worried by her mental state than she appeared to be. The sessions became increasingly boring. (Let us not pretend that patients can and do not bore us – indeed, for those of us who have been in therapy, no doubt we have all been boring to our own analysts and therapists!)

One evening I was driving home at about ten past six when I realised that Deirdre had a six o'clock appointment. I rushed back to the hospital where the kindly elderly porter told me, 'Your patient came but I told her that you had gone home.' Instantly, I realised that I had allowed the treatment to break down and that normal rules did not apply. I phoned her flat but there was no reply. I attempted to go round to the house, but again there was no response to my ringing the bell. Not knowing what to do in this crisis of my own making, I left her a note saying that I would see her at nine o'clock the next morning.

The following morning I was greeted by the news that my patient was unconscious and on a respirator having taken a large overdose of barbiturates. She remained on the respirator for a further day. Despite severe complications from the overdose, she recovered consciousness. I went to see her on the medical ward and asked her if she had got my note. She replied, 'Yes, but you'd done it by then'. It transpired that what I had done was to act out her most feared fantasy of rejection and abandonment, and she had made me do it. Although she had contributed to and in large measure contrived her own rejection, I had been the executioner and felt justly guilty.

She returned to treatment, which now was far from boring. We explored at great length the trap into which she had unknowingly led me, and my part in being the aloof and negligent parent who failed her when put to the test. She continued to see me for a further year and a half, and left to take up training in another part of the country. I believe she did well.

A couple of years later I received a card – unsigned but undoubtedly from her – which said, 'At times like this, it's good to know you're still alive'. She was going through another crisis and needed to know that she had not killed me off.

To return to our central theme in this section, the therapist must be aware that if they take someone on for therapy following a suicide attempt and after a gap, or referred "second hand" from another clinician, they may be implicated in another suicide attempt. Indeed, this may be a necessary part of the therapeutic process; a daunting prospect, but a real one. It also emphasises the importance of continuity and reliability for the suicidal individual.

The painful reality, which every therapist needs to come to terms with, is the fact that it is always within the patient's power to kill themselves. Even permanent incarceration may not prevent a successful suicidal act. It is well known that suicides all too often occur in psychiatric institutions. There may come a time in the therapy that the therapist has to communicate this reality to the suicidal patient. This statement to the patient in no way implies that the therapist does not care or condones suicide. On the contrary, it implies that the patient will only move on from the suicidal state of mind if the therapist can take the risk of letting the patient be responsible for his or her own life. Psychic change can only take place when the patient is free to act and the analyst is free to analyse. If either the patient or the analyst is operating under external pressure, coercion or moral blackmail, the best that can be hoped for is compliance rather than real permanent psychic change. It is equally important that, within the therapeutic relationship, the therapist does not pressure the patient to change. Only then can the patient start to relinquish his or her own murderous fantasies. Recognising and explicitly exploring with the patient their murderousness and the impact that suicide would have on the therapist provides the patient with an opportunity to open up to that part of themselves that wants to live.

It is a matter of fine judgement as to whether the patient is able to take responsibility for his or her own life at any specific point in time. If all or most of the warning signals previously described are evident, the patient is clearly in the pre-suicidal stage of the process. This is most obvious when the person is in a clearly psychotic state as judged in conventional psychiatric terms. Usually, however, the person is not overtly psychotic and the problem becomes to determine how much the person's thinking and feeling is dominated by suicidal impulses. The patient will seek to reassure the professional that suicide will not happen, but the explicit promise that the person will not try to kill themselves should be treated with extreme caution; suicidal impulses are devious and can trick both the person themselves and the professional wishing to help. To renounce the option of suicide is to lose a crucial sense of potency and self-efficacy.

Case study: Taking responsibility for a body that has been attacked

An example from a colleague, Mike Shooter, which is quoted with his permission, elegantly makes the point that, to improve, the patient has to take responsibility for their body; the body they have attacked. Many years ago Mike Shooter was running an outpatient group for adolescents.

During a group therapy session, a girl left the group, went to the lavatory and returned to the group having cut her wrists. She demanded to be taken to the casualty department.

Having established that her wounds were not immediately life threatening, the therapist took the risk that the patient was ready and suggested to the group that they give the patient the responsibility of taking herself to the casualty department. This she did and returned to the group and made good use of the experience. Ten years later she committed suicide. The therapist decided to go to the funeral. There were few close relatives. He approached an aunt who he knew had been the closest to her and said to her, 'I feel I let your niece down by not looking after her'. 'Oh no,' replied the aunt, 'you gave her another ten years of life'. Whether, in the risk-aversive culture which now dominates our practice, he would dare take the same risk, Mike Shooter has his doubts. This case vignette also makes the point that the option of suicide is often revived by the patient as a solution to future crises.

The aftermath of completed suicide

Little can prepare the professional for the experience of losing a patient by suicide. We employ all our customary professional and personal defences such as denial, displacement, black humour, intellectualisation and medicalisation to protect ourselves from the pain. For a fuller account see Hale and Hudson (as cited in Brownscombe Heller & Pollet, 2010). We are faced with failure, impotence, guilt, sadness, the fear that we will be criticised by our peers or an enquiry for having failed in our professional duty or judgement. Depressive and paranoid guilt ensues. It is then that we realise how much we need supportive and honest colleagues. The value of the psychological post mortem cannot be overemphasised: a process in which all those professionals who have been involved in the patient's care meet in a structured setting to trace the events which have led up to the patient's death and to try to make some sense of them. Colleagues may feel that they have contributed by acts both of omission and commission. Suicide is never a single person's fault or the fault of a single organisation. Responsibility should not be avoided but it should not be a persecution. Perhaps, more importantly, it is an opportunity to express our anger, sadness and puzzlement – indeed, probably all the feelings that led the individual to commit suicide. It is our experience that our institutions and we are permanently affected by a patient's suicide. We can learn from the experience and move on. But can we, or indeed should we, ever forget?

The impact of a suicide on the professional

There are two events which we, as professionals, dread; that a patient in our care commits a serious crime such as killing another or serious sexual assault, or that they kill themselves. Practically all of us are likely to have a patient commit suicide at some point in our professional careers, yet it is remarkable how, with a few noticeable exceptions, there is so little written about the subject. This is particularly true in the UK literature (with the exception of the article by Foley and Kelly (2007) and Brigg's chapter in *Relating to Self-Harm and Suicide* (2008)), but also in the American literature; but even in the US they comment on the paucity of literature and discussion. It is as though the act itself paralyses us. Our patients elect us to be the current representation of their primary carer; in suicide, it is the primary carer who is the object of attack. We too are the recipients of a professional and personal attack. Our professional defensive structures, both individual and collective, are laid asunder; our core selves are exposed and tortured. We experience all the emotions which drove the individual to suicide – pain, anger, loss, despair, guilt, uncertainty and, if we are honest, we may experience a sense of relief.

As with any countertransference reaction, what we experience is a combination, an interaction of, on the one hand, feelings projected into us by the patient derived from their unconscious, and on the other hand, our own emotional structure and experience located largely in our unconscious. Thus, our propensity to anxiety, depression and feelings of guilt will to an extent determine our reaction; it is significant, however, that Hendin, Lipschitz, Maltsberger, Haas and Wynecoop (2000) found in their survey of therapists who had experienced a patient suicide that 'the intensity of the therapists' emotional response was independent of the therapists' age, years of experience or practice setting'.

Given that the reactions to suicide are so personal and so profound, the material used in this chapter is itself intentionally personal. In this regard we have used the papers by Gitlin (1999) and Hendin et al. (2000). We have also used material from the monthly meetings of five consultant psychiatrists who have met for the past three years to discuss current episodes of suicidality and completed suicide.

Looking at the reactions described by professionals, a remarkably consistent pattern emerges akin to the normal process of mourning but with its own particular features. Of course, the impact on the professional is far less than the life-long devastation imposed on those in a close loving relationship with the victim; for them the sadomasochistic elements of the relationship are frozen at their zenith.

Personal reactions to the death by suicide of one's patient

Chronologically, the first reaction to learning of a patient's suicide is often a sense of numbness, particularly when an event relating to the suicide provokes sudden anxiety. This is, of course, normal in any form of bereavement. Connected to it is a sense of disbelief and depersonalisation, as though the clinician were acting normal whilst internally totally preoccupied and in turmoil.

Shame rapidly invades the mind – that they alone are the only ones who had a patient commit suicide and that henceforth they would be regarded by their colleagues as deficient therapists who had brought dishonour on themselves and on their profession, effectively blighting their careers henceforth. Whilst it may seem that these responses are extreme, feared fantasies are made up of the extreme. Thus far the concern is for the self, but after a short time a sense of sadness and grief at the loss of the relationship starts to appear, paralleling the feelings of pain of relatives and friends experiencing such a bereavement. Perhaps perplexingly, both therapist and relatives are invaded by a sense of anger which in its own right induces internal conflict and further guilt: 'Should I be having these feelings?'. It is here that the fantasy of sadomasochistic revenge inherent in the suicidal act must be recognised in order to understand that the anger felt by the 'survivors' is the anger which, in part, drove the person to suicide. Indeed, it is the failure on the part of the suicidal individual to recognise their own anger which leads them to act it out on their own body and to destroy, perhaps forever, the mental equilibrium of the survivors. 'The young person knows that thereby he will inflict the greatest pain' (Stekel, 1910). Yet by attacking himself, the individual seemingly deprives us of the entitlement to anger.

The fear of condemnation by colleagues gives a sense of public humiliation, which merges into a fear of being sued. Such thoughts lead to brooding about the documentation of the case, checking the notes and questioning all the decisions made in the patient's care. The 'court' is within the therapist's mind, though the process may later be enacted in the coroner's court. These thoughts take hold of the therapist's conscious and preconscious mind – endless circular ruminations and self-accusations disturbing sleep and relentlessly pursuing the therapist in the wee small hours of the night. Clinical judgement may now become distorted with the overvaluation of suicidal potential and an avoidance of such patients. Each unexpected phone call causes the stomach to lurch in anticipation of another disaster. It is, in effect, post-traumatic stress disorder with all the manifestations we recognise in our patients but perhaps are reluctant to acknowledge in ourselves.

Central to the experience is the sense that we as therapists have failed, not only in the eyes of others but also in our own eyes. Our professional identity and the reason we went into psychiatry has been attacked and invalidated. Within it is the experience that we have been tricked by the patient. We have been lulled into a sense of false security by the patient who then has triumphantly shown our inadequacy to recognise their suicidal potential or to prevent them from killing him or herself and thus, part of us, in the process. Our therapeutic power (and in it our therapeutic narcissism) has been shown to be for naught. The patient's wish for self-destruction has been greater than our capacity to keep them alive. In killing themselves they have won the sadomasochistic battle but paradoxically have lost their lives. We, and the relatives, are the survivors, albeit permanently damaged by the experience.

Our relationships with our colleagues alter too; we compare ourselves unfavourably with those who have not lost a patient through suicide, and we look for solace to those whom we know have been through the same trauma. In our personal relationships we may become more withdrawn and private, preoccupied with our guilt for what has happened and anxious about what may come. We have, in effect, become depressed. Of course, various defensive mechanisms may diminish our feelings of distress; the two most commonly employed by the ego being denial and rationalisation/intellectualisation. The changes to our practice may be appropriate but may also be seen as an acting out in the countertransference of the anxieties provoked by the suicide and an overreaction if we alter the management of all patients based on the experience with one. We, and the system, become risk averse, the result being that we are reluctant to take the calculated risks that are necessary if our patients are to become able to take responsibility for their own lives. Our (over) reactions are seen by Gitlin (1999) as 'the need to maintain one's illusion of control in an unpredictable world in order to bind anxiety' and the ritualistic enquiries of every patient as a form of magical thinking that will reassert our control. Perhaps this also explains the emphasis on the process of 'risk assessment', often of a formulaic form filling, but which it would appear from recent research (Troquete, Van den Brink, Bientema & Mulder, 2013) offers no benefit to the management of the patient, certainly as far as violence towards others is concerned.

Working through the tortured feelings following a patient's suicide is a long and often lonely process, but it is surely here that one's colleagues should be of help. However, all too often the professional is reluctant to share the feelings, either out of a sense of shame or machismo – 'these things don't worry me, they're just part of the job'. Also there is the fear that other professionals will not want to hear one's distress, an experience sometimes born out in reality. For those who are in therapy or analysis, the professional may derive considerable support by being able to stay with the pain, tolerate it and put it into some perspective. Consulting a senior respected psychotherapist colleague for a limited number of sessions on a personal and confidential basis can serve the same function. Through it all it is crucial to recognise that one has been damaged by the patient's suicide and one needs time and space to heal. This process is very hard if you are under the threat of legal proceedings, which may trigger paranoid thinking and self-justification.

When a suicide has occurred within an institution we strongly recommend a psychiatric post mortem for all the professionals involved to examine the events and the roles of staff and the institution as a whole, because splitting and the ascribing of blame to others, particularly if they are not there, can take place all too easily. In our experience, this process can be facilitated by an external consultant with experience of working with suicide – the members of staff then feel it safer to explore the territory. The timing of this intervention is, as Goldstein and Buongiorno (1984) point out, important. If intervention is too soon, the personal experience of loss, anger and guilt may be prematurely suppressed and replaced by an intellectual understanding, albeit that this may be appropriate later. Most institutions only set up such meetings on an 'ad hoc' basis, but we have found that it is useful to have a regular monthly meeting, acknowledging that suicide or the threat of suicide are constantly with us in clinical practice.

Reflecting the importance of this group, the remainder of this chapter is a joint effort of the five of us. The group consists of four consultant psychiatrists – Rachel Gibbons, Siobhan Jeffrey, Nora Turjanski and Nisha Shah, with Rob Hale as the facilitator. We have been meeting monthly for the past four years.

The response within the institution

Clinicians involved and working closely with a patient who commits suicide often feel overwhelmed not only by the internal experience but also by the subsequent institutional response. In the three months after a suicide, an organisation within the National Health Service usually conducts a Serious Incident Inquiry (Serious Untoward Incident – SUI). This is an investigation that varies in its degree of intensity depending on the circumstances surrounding the death and the internal policies of the organisation. The panel examines the notes and interviews the clinicians involved. They produce a report which will be sent to the coroner as well as the relatives and may be circulated to all other senior clinicians within the organisation. This investigation can be considered a reasonable response of a public organisation where the task is to learn from mistakes. It is an approach that has been reported to improve safety in other branches of medicine and industry.

However, the clinicians experience of this investigation rarely feels like a dispassionate factual analysis of the circumstances surrounding the care of the patient: a 'learn from mistakes' assessment. Instead, it is often experienced as a difficult and persecutory process, unlike the root cause analysis of other serious incidents. Small wonder when one considers that one of the unconscious purposes of the suicidal individual's act is to make others feel guilty, be they relatives, friends or particularly professionals. Accidents and illnesses can be perceived as caused by external circumstances and outside the control of the individual; not so suicide – the individual has consciously inflicted death.

Not surprisingly, the impact on the organisation is peculiar to suicide and unlike other deaths. Whereas the impact on the individual clinician may be obvious, the impact on the structure and functioning of the unit may be more opaque. Each of us as clinicians will in part inevitably seek unconsciously to exonerate ourselves and project our internal sense of blame and responsibility on to others. The institution, as with any group, will find its vulnerability exposed, and unconscious retributive sadism may be excited and scapegoating ensue in order to get rid of the institutional responsibility. Inevitably this will lead to splits in the functioning of the organisation. Thus, clinicians, already overwhelmed by guilt and internally persecuted, now feel accused and on trial in front of their own organisation. The internal ruminations over a perceived 'fatal mistake' may now result in a masochistic presentation to the panel and the possibility of volunteering for being the scapegoat.

A powerful underlying assumption of this review panel is frequently that a flaw or imperfection in the patient's care was the cause of the suicide. Whilst it may be that there have been mistakes, it is important to recognise that secrecy and deception concerning suicidal intent are frequently an integral part of the suicidal process, a theme explored elsewhere in this book. This whole process can lead to the clinician feeling let down and unprotected by their organisation. On one hand, they are encouraged to 'positive risk-take', and on the other hand, they find themselves accused and blamed when the risks materialise. This breakdown in the internal relationship the clinician has with her/his organisation leads to disaffection, reduced engagement with patients and the institutional task, and can result in early retirement. Obviously, this is not always the case and a well conducted, supportive and compassionate investigation can result in a positive experience, which enables professional growth and helps process the feelings of guilt and distress.

The coroner's court

The coroner's inquest may happen months or even years after the suicide. Virtually all suicide inquests require the clinician to attend. The time leading to the court appearance is difficult. There is the frightening feeling of attending a trial with the perceived risk of public humiliation and exposure of personal flaws, even reported in the newspapers. The reality of the inquest gets distorted by the projection of the internal psychic court or superego into this external experience as well as the external realities. The advantage of the delay between suicide and court appearance is that generally by the time the clinician attends the inquest he will have moved into a more reality based internal dialogue in touch with the role of a balanced and resilient witness.

The actual reality of the experience of attending the coroner's court will depend on a variety of factors: the factors surrounding the suicide, the position taken by the organisation, the views and attitudes of the relatives, and, not least, by the coroner him or herself. We, the members of the group, have had widely differing experiences, but in general we have found it relieving to put down the burden we have had to carry since the suicide. Often, when all the evidence comes together in the court it emerges that the clinicians and the organisation have played a relatively small role in the events leading up to the suicide. We should have regard, however, for the possibility that there may be divergence between the interests of the individual clinician and the organisation within which they are working, and it is often wise to seek the opinion of a professional indemnity organisation where possible. That said, it is generally a time for closure and in some instances the process has enabled a rapprochement with the family who have been angry and blaming beforehand.

A suicide is often followed by a profound sense of psychological pain, effectively post-traumatic stress disorder, which distorts the clinician's view of him or herself and their clinical practice for a long period afterwards. Each new suicide rekindles the trauma of a previous suicide, and the evidence suggests that it does not lose its intensity with seniority. Deaths of terminally ill patients are taken as part of medicine. This is not so in psychiatry and particularly in death from suicide. The reasons are complex but it is clear that suicide leaves a psychic mark on all of us.

References

Alvarez, A. (1974). *The savage god*. Harmondsworth, England: Penguin Books Ltd.

Asch, S. S. (1980). Suicide, and the hidden executioner. *International Review of Psycho-Analysis, 7*, 51–60.

Briggs, S., Lemma, A. & Crouch, W. (Eds.) (2008), *Relating to self-harm and suicide: Psychoanalytic perspectives on practice, theory and prevention*. New York, NY US: Routledge/Taylor & Francis Group.

Brownscombe Heller, M. & Pollet, S. (2010). The work of psychoanalysts in the public health sector. New York: Routledge/Taylor and Francis Group.

Foley, S. & Kelly, B. (2007). When a patient dies by suicide; incidence, implications and coping strategies. *Advances in Psychiatric Treatment, 13*, 134–138.

Gitlin, M. J. (1999). A psychiatrist's reaction to a patient's suicide. *The American Journal of Psychiatry, 156*(10), 1630–1634.

Goldstein, L. S. & Buongiorno, P. A. (1984). Psychotherapists as suicide survivors. *American Journal of Psychotherapy, 38*(3), 392–398.

Gutheil, E. (1948). Dream and suicide. *American Journal of Psychotherapy, 2*, 283–294.

Gutheil, E. A. (1999). Dream and suicide. *American Journal of Psychotherapy, 53*(2), 246–257.

Hawton, K. & Fagg, J. (1988). Suicide, and other causes of death, following attempted suicide. *The British Journal of Psychiatry, 152*, 359–366. doi: 10.1192/bjp.152.3.359

Hendin, H., Lipschitz, A., Maltsberger, J. T., Haas, A. P. & Wynecoop, S. (2000). Therapists' reactions to patients' suicides. *The American Journal of Psychiatry, 157*(12), 2022–2027. doi: 10.1176/appi.ajp.157.12.2022

Lukaschek, K., Baumert, J., Krawitz, M., Erazo, N., Forsti, H. & Ladwig, K. H. (2014). Determinants of completed railway suicides by psychiatric inpatients: Case control study. *British Journal of Psychiatry, 205,* 398–406.

NICE. (2004). Self harm: The short term physical and psychological management and secondary prevention of self harm in primary and secondary care. London: NICE

Richman, J. (1986). *Family therapy for suicidal people.* New York: Springer.

Richman, J. & Rosenbaum, M. (1970). A clinical study of the role of hostility and death wishes by the family and society in suicidal attempts. *Israel Annals of Psychiatry and Related Disciplines, 8,* 213–231.

Richman, J. & Rosenbaum, M. (1996). A clinical study of the role of hostility and death wishes by the family and society in suicidal attempts. In J. T. Maltsberger & M. J. Goldblatt (Eds.), *Essential papers on suicide.* (pp. 221–242). New York, NY US: New York University Press.

Stekel, W. (1910). Symposium on Suicide. *On suicide* (pp. 33–141). New York: International Universities Press.

Straker, M. (1958). Clinical observations of suicide. *Canadian Medical Association Journal, 79,* 473–479.

Tahka, V. A. (1978). On some narcissistic aspect of self-destructive behaviour and their influence on its predicatability. *Psychiatra Fennica Supplementum,* 59–62.

Troquete, N., Van den Brink, R., Bientema, H. & Mulder, T. (2013). Controlled risk assessment and shared care planning in an outpatient forensic psychiatry: Cluster randomised trial. *British Journal of Psychiatry, 202,* 365–371.

Chapter 10

Self-mutilation

Self-mutilation is an act aimed at damaging and torturing the self's body to torture the mind of the other. By contrast, suicide aims to kill the self's body to create a permanent epitaph in the mind of the other. Although they have certain elements in common, it is an important distinction to make for three reasons: first, in descriptive terms, the two acts present different profiles not least of which is the outcome; second, because each leads to a different countertransference experience in professionals and relatives; and, third, and most importantly, the patients themselves clearly make the distinction, particularly if on some occasions they self-mutilate and on others attempt suicide. In an unpublished study using grounded theory (a systematic methodology in social sciences involving the discovery of theory through the analysis of data), MacCarthy quotes from a patient in the research illustrating the last point: 'Cutting has never been about trying to kill myself; it's about cutting myself. To make me feel better, you know' (C. MacCarthy, personal communication, April 01, 2006).

The act in which the differentiation is less clear is the tying of ligatures around the neck, which has elements of both. Is there a continuum with suicide at one end and self-mutilation at the other, with self-strangulation lying half way along? Or should this be regarded as a separate phenomenon perhaps more akin to the 'addiction to near death' described by Joseph (1982).

A word about definitions. Within the literature the terminology is confusing. A frequently used term is 'self-harm'; this can be taken as meaning any attack generally on the self whether suicidal or non-suicidal in intent, or it can mean more specifically cutting or burning of the body without suicidal intent (conscious or unconscious). The term 'self-wounding' is also used which encompasses the wish to alter or disfigure the body as well as the wish to damage and inflict pain. Sometimes within a paper or report it is not clear what is being referred to; this is particularly apparent when the conceptual framework does not espouse the concept of unconscious motivation or countertransference. What we are concerned with here are individuals who, often repetitively, inflict wounds on their bodies typically by cutting with a knife or razor blade, or by burning typically with a cigarette. For this, we use the term 'self-mutilation'; we see these acts as different from those where the individual cuts or burns their body with the intention of putting their life in danger. An example of the latter would be a patient, himself a doctor, who locked himself in the lavatory, dissected out each brachial artery, (the main blood vessel supplying the arm), and cut it longitudinally. This was no 'delicate self-cutting'. Amazingly, he survived, much to his disappointment and fury; killing and death had been his intention. Equally, there are individuals who carry out acts which disfigure their bodies or they get others to carry out such acts; of these we have little clinical experience.

Our purpose in this section is not to provide a comprehensive clinical study of self-mutilation but to explore some of the psychoanalytically based literature and concepts about the phenomena. We will, of course, also be drawing on some of our own clinical experience. What is immediately clear is that self-mutilation is a highly complex and over determined phenomenon containing many contradictions. As with suicide, it is triggered by current events but the motive force is the stimulation of unresolved traumatic experiences of infancy and childhood, which are themselves unconsciously represented and temporarily reversed by the act; in a sense it is a 'recovered memory'.

We adopt a developmental and object relations model in order to consider each libidinal stage and to assign each of the phenomena to a specific stage. Overall, we see acts of self-mutilation as instantaneous and simultaneous returns to various levels of primitive functioning (regression).

Let us consider each separately. The most primitive regressive state is of being in undifferentiated fusion with the primary object, the very early caregiver, typically the mother. In the act of self-mutilation the blood is experienced as warm, comforting and alive – a consanguinity with the mother's blood before any separation occurred. The same oceanic bliss we encountered in suicide but achieved by different means.

The normal oral stage involves the process of gradual disillusionment – the safe movement towards separation, with the mother recognising and modulating the infant's anxiety and anger, following the cues of her child and not imposing her own agenda on the child. Nonetheless, the child inevitably and necessarily experiences the mother as idealised or disappointing, but in 'copeable' quantities.

The experience of a self-mutilator is very different. These are the children of mothers who were by turns narcissistically self-absorbed and unavailable for their child, or needing to control their child by self-serving domination, which is often avaricious, penetrating and malevolent. Core Complex anxieties are thus created – abandonment to starve or intrusive annihilation. Gardner (2001) describes this as an 'encaptive' conflict in which, as adults (or adolescents) individuals are still captivated by the need for the mother and simultaneously desperate to break free from these malevolent bonds.

Skin is the medium for the self-mutilating act. Biven (1977; 2005) uses the term 'envelopment' to describe a Core Complex dynamic in Kenny, a self-mutilating adolescent patient who sealed a plastic bag over his head. When he began to lose consciousness, Kenny would make an incision close to his mouth and take deep gasps of air. The bag appeared to function as a substitute skin, which Kenny could mutilate and escape from (2005, p. 62). Biven illustrates the ambivalently cathected nature of skin in the self-mutilating act with reference to an ancient Aztec ritual of priests who 'dressed' in the skin of sacrificial victims who had been endowed with omnipotent powers before their sacrifice. While the priests were 'wearing' the skin they felt themselves to be the god Xipe, the Flayed One (p. 64). However, like Kenny, the priests could also escape when the skin was taken off after 20 days. Biven's anthropological reference illuminates the psychic overlap between cross-dressing, transvestism, transsexualism, mutilation and self-mutilation, and the potential for the development (unconsciously) of a structured sexual perversion which maintains a contact with the object but repels any real intimacy. Self-mutilation can be seen as providing the same dual function but in an 'acute' and temporary way.

Whereas suicide is more frequently triggered by just the loss of, or rejection by, the object, self-mutilation is triggered by both anxieties – rejection and intrusion experienced simultaneously. In the act of self-mutilation the object (now the therapist or the institution) is both sought and clung to in desperate need, and at the same time attacked in violent reprisal and to escape the intrusive control. A countertransference reaction or the professional's 'affective response' (King, 1978) confirms this *confusion* of purposes. Our perception is that the patient desperately needs us but alienates us and prevents us from providing anything beneficial. Our self-mutilating patients communicate with us not by request (which runs the risk of being refused) or affection but by coercion and cruelty because their experience is that they cannot – dare not – trust. If we are not careful, our response as therapists is, in turn, not to trust them.

In this regressive state there is no capacity in the patient to tolerate powerful negative affect. However, the patient also hopes that there will be someone who can understand the meaning of the attack on the body, rather than just reacting to it, and thus offer an opportunity for containment and resolution. But self-mutilation is a pathological solution, not only because of its temporary nature but also, crucially, it makes things worse rather than better.

Another facet of this very early developmental stage is the importance of the skin as a medium for affectionate and soothing communication through tactile experience; in self-mutilation this medium is used but in a primarily destructive and painful way. For a more detailed study of this aspect see Motz (2010a).

The anal phase, which follows the oral phase, is essentially about the child gradually taking ownership of its own body and gaining control of its bodily functions, particularly those concerned with the excretion and elimination of urine and faeces. There is an emphasis on delineating that which is nurturing from that which is toxic and thus to be eliminated; the physiological response to the toxicity (of faeces in particular) is nausea. The child controls his objects (people) by the control of these excretory functions, complying with or resisting parental demands. In adolescence and adulthood self-mutilation again attempts to assert this control in an omnipotent and remorseless way. Furthermore, the wounds are themselves revolting; the creation of nausea in the object is a means of inflicting revenge and triumphantly controlling the object. This need to control is exemplified in the repetitive and ritualistic character of much self-mutilation with great attention to fine detail which can at times have an almost magical quality to it. Motz (2010b) quotes from Caroline Kettlewell's memoir *Skin Game* (2000).

In the razor's wake, the skin melted away, parted to show briefly the milky white subcutaneous layers before a thin beaded line of rich crimson blood seeped through the inch-long divide. Then the blood welled up and began to distort the pure, stark edges of my delicately wrought wound. The chaos in my head spun itself into a silk of silence. I had distilled myself to the immediacy of hand, blade, blood, flesh (p. 27).

To the outsider, the reaction to such a description is similar to the revulsion experienced upon hearing about a perverse act, whereas to the self-mutilator the act is exciting and pleasurable.

Self-mutilation also has addictive qualities; it was noted by Coid, Allolio and Rees in 1983 that the act was accompanied by raised plasma endorphin levels – the body's naturally occurring opiates. They saw this as the result of the tissue damage. However, people who self-mutilate will often tell you that they experienced the endorphin high before cutting or burning themselves. This has two results: first, the physical pain is not experienced, and second, the psychological experience is of elation, sexual excitement and relaxation of superego control. It is often said that the superego is that part of the mind which is soluble in alcohol; perhaps it is also soluble in endorphins.

The child's move to accepting their own genitality and thence to Oedipal functioning involves the safe exploration and enjoyment of their own sexuality with the parent of the opposite sex. For the self-mutilator this is often 'a bridge too far'. Many are pathologically stuck in unresolved oral and Oedipal conflicts; others, if they do dare to entertain Oedipal fantasies may have them distorted by actual sexual abuse with its ensuing (and totally undeserved) guilt. Not only does the self-mutilation seek to exonerate the guilt by self-punishment, it also replaces the unbearable pain of guilt with a more bearable physical pain. An important fantasy driving the act is self-purification – the toxicity of the sexual abuse must be eliminated from the body.

> The pain becomes unbearable and you cut to see blood. I was always convinced that inside me was green mucus. So, instead of blood, I would have filth and snot in my veins. And sometimes you would hear this voice saying 'you're dirty, you're muck' and you just slash… . anything to prove it's blood.
>
> (McCarthy, 2006)

Small wonder then that so many retreat from true sexual identity and sexual functioning, although this may only become apparent at puberty. It is remarkable how many self-mutilators have either an asexual appearance or one of exaggerated and superficial sexuality.

Perhaps the purest form of the act is genital self-mutilation, and all other cuttings and burnings represent displacement from genital self-mutilation. It also may unconsciously create a vagina – Caroline Kettlewell's 'inch long divide' (Kettlewell, 2000).

> Years ago, when I was younger, I would wash my vulva and vagina with a nail brush, which is very, very painful, until it bled which didn't take that long. I would bathe it in bleach ... just put it into my hands and rub it into areas until it burned. But once I discovered cutting I didn't need to do that anymore.
>
> (McCarthy, 2006)

Displaying the wounds, having them recognised and tended to by medical or nursing staff, is an important part of the cycle. Sometimes the opposite is true – the wounds are kept secret often to fester and prolong the process of suffering; they may also actively interfere with the healing process, inserting foreign objects into the wound. Sometimes a patient will encourage the attending doctor to suture without an anaesthetic, drawing the doctor into collusion with further damage. In the longer term, the wounds may be a source of shame, guilt and embarrassment to be kept covered from the view of others. Equally they may be openly displayed as stigmata of past and present suffering.

From this description a model of the underlying psychodynamics can be adduced. The mother is (unconsciously) experienced as by turns rejecting and insensitive to the child's needs, and by turns intrusive and controlling; furthermore, she is perceived as concerned with her own hyper-femininity, competing with the child's (self-mutilators are more commonly female) sense of femininity and depriving the child of the opportunity to identify with the mother. The father is absent or, more likely, abusive in a sexual or violent way, unable to protect her from the mother's entrapment. The individual grows up typically both with an impoverished sense of being cared for and of their sexuality being devalued.

As in suicide, the current precipitant to self-mutilation is customarily seen as separation, perceived by the individual as abandonment. However, the longed for closeness is as dangerous, if not more so because the object can so easily be perceived as intrusive and annihilatory. Perhaps the most dangerous situation for the individual is to experience both (oral) anxieties simultaneously and in an undifferentiated way, despite the fact that they are opposites. The loss of control over external circumstances, particularly where rivalry for attention and affection is concerned, is a powerful and necessary component.

Turning to sexuality, apparently normal femininity in the other can be experienced as magnetically tantalising but essentially capricious and untrustworthy. When there has been overt and consciously remembered sexual abuse by a 'trusted' male, masculinity in the other is experienced as distantly appealing but actually abusive, serving the other's needs and exploiting the individual's neediness. Not surprisingly, often relationships with males are insignificant or almost discounted.

These three sets of precipitants gain their power not from the current situation, but because they mimic and thus stimulate the largely unconscious unresolved oral, anal and Oedipal conflicts and fantasies previously described. Obviously where anxieties from all three levels are stimulated the threat is maximal. The apparent solution is that provided by the symbolic act of self-mutilation with all its carefully crafted components; but it is a pathological solution because it is temporary, it alienates sources of support and it fails to resolve any of the underlying conflicts.

Within a closed institution such as a (women's) secure unit or prison the effect of these dynamics on the staff can be dramatic. The act of self-mutilation stimulates in us as professional staff simultaneous and diametrically opposed emotions – protective concern versus dismissive anger, cynicism and reprisal, affection versus revulsion. Our minds struggle, and frequently fail, to make sense of these contradictory experiences reflecting as they do the experiences of the patient. The professional's burnt out state of mind may function to remove them from situations that are felt to be traumatic. But we can ultimately walk away from the conflict and find space and other relationships to help us recover.

The patient has no such option.

In therapy with patients who were searching for sexual reassignment surgery (SRS), we found that several of them had displaced their impulses to mutilate themselves onto surgeons, so that one component of their fantasy was self-mutilation by proxy. Both the self-mutilator and those mutilating by proxy projected rage against the mother onto the body. Perhaps paradoxically, these patients who were pursing SRS often identified the surgeon with their mother who they felt hated their masculine body. Alessandra Lemma's (2015) clinical work with patients who requested SRS found that beneath the delusion that gender could, in fact, be 'assigned' surgically through SRS, these patients had found a way of representing, unconsciously, the incongruity of the subject's gender identity.

References

Biven, B. (1977) A violent solution: The role of skin in a severe adolescent regression. In *Psychoanal Study Child*, *32*, 327–352. And (2005) *True pretences*. Leicester: Matador, pp. 48–69.

Campbell, D. (2015) Foreword, In *Minding the body*. London: Routledge, pp. xv–xxvi.

Coid, J., Allolio, B. & Rees, L. H. (1983). Raised plasma metenkephalin in patients who habitually mutilate themselves. *Lancet, 2*(8349), 545–546.

Gardner, F. (2001). *Self-harm: A psychotherapeutic approach*. New York, NY US: Brunner-Routledge.

Joseph, B. (1982). Addiction to near-death. *International Journal of Psycho-Analysis, 63*, 449–456.

Kettlewell, C. (2000). *Skin game*. New York: Griffin.

King, P. (1978). Affective response of the analyst to the patient's communications. *The International Journal of Psychoanalysis, 59*(2-3), 329–334.

Lemma, A. *Minding the body*. London: Routledge.

McCarthy, C (2006) Personal communication.

Motz, A. (2010a). Self-harm as a sign of hope. *Psychoanalytic Psychotherapy, 24*(2), 81–92. doi: 10.1080/02668731003707527

Motz, A. (2010b). *Managing self harm*. New York: Routledge, Taylor & Francis Group.

Chapter 11

A patient's account

The account we have given in this book is essentially that of two professionals observing and trying to make sense of self-destructive acts. Although we have studied the psychoanalytic literature on suicide, we cannot underestimate what we have learned from our patients and their experiences of suicide. It is for this reason that we conclude with this personal account by one of our patients, which was written when she finished her analysis, revised a few years later for this publication, and is printed here with her permission.

Case study: Learning from a suicide attempt

I tried to commit suicide when I was 22, although I had experienced intermittent severe depression for at least six years previously, with one seriously suicidal period in my mid-teens. This was at the age of 16 when, overwhelmed with misery at the break-up with my first boyfriend, I thought of suicide every night for some months. I stood by my bedroom window every evening and tried to pluck up the courage to jump. Fear and some stubborn, residual hope prevented me from acting, although that failure – as I saw it – also plunged me back into the original state of paralysing misery, which had given rise to my suicidal impulse in the first place.

Nonetheless, there was also something assuaging in the nightly ritual, to do with the feeling that I had an escape route – a dangerous thought that stayed with me. These suicidal fantasies also, importantly, gave me a temporary sense of control in the face of overwhelming and frightening feelings – paradoxically a sense of identity, personal agency and emotional 'coherence' – in other words, a distorted attempt at emotional repair. I now think this period was not merely a discrete rehearsal for my actual suicide attempt later, but in a psychic continuum with it, containing both the destructive forces which led to that attempt and the creative energies which permitted me to emerge into greater health once I had the necessary help. I think, in fact, any 'suicide' involves tremendous energies and so, the potential for immense personal transformation, but only if skilled, intensive help can be accessed.

I think that, lacking fundamental emotional engagement with my mother, I had been suicidal at some level since my childhood. The children of the family were not encouraged to express or share emotion, and any negative feelings were greeted with impatience or outright anger, with only intermittent and unpredictable parental affection shown (this is a pale description of an often anguishing situation in which the keynote for all siblings was a great loneliness and fearfulness and elements of rage). The emotional vacuum and the sense of helplessness this engendered are difficult to describe to anyone who has not experienced something similar (plants with their roots groping in air).

Despite the family embargo on emotional revelation, as my depression at 16 persisted, I had just enough detachment to realise that I desperately needed help. Despite my familiarity with frequent depressions (which I thought of as something almost normal), this was the most extreme and prolonged period I had ever experienced. I felt completely alone and helpless, as well as frightened at the extremity of my own grief. I asked my parents if I could see a psychiatrist, who was the only kind of 'mind doctor' I had heard of. They refused, almost certainly because of the sense of stigma attached to anything concerned with psychiatry for their generation, and probably because they were understandably frightened at the evidence of something so awry in the family, and even angry at the reproach inherent in my request.

I did not know of any agencies that could help me (it was the early seventies and I suppose there were fewer outlets for young people, or that they were less well publicised). And there was certainly no one at school I could have talked to confidentially.

It was only the strong affection and support of one of my sisters which saw me through this period, but, although endlessly patient, she was fundamentally puzzled by my state and helpless to alter it significantly.

It was the failure of another relationship – one in a series – at 22 years old which precipitated a serious attempt to kill myself by swallowing 70 aspirins, a carefully premeditated step, when I had moved beyond persistent depression into despair. I differentiate the two in the hope that anyone reading this, whether professionals or individuals similarly afflicted, will understand that suicide is a process in which *intervention – and hence prevention – is always possible, but timing is crucial.*

Suicidal thoughts, as at other traumatic periods of perceived abandonment, obsessed me after this particular break-up, and I carefully bought two bottles of aspirins at separate shops to avoid suspicion and hid them. At this stage, as until almost the final day of the attempt, my feelings were ambivalent: I wanted to die and I wanted desperately to be rescued, so that even after buying the aspirins, I continued to make plans for my next university term.

However, I remained in a state of alternating active grief with a terrifying sense of solitude, and a paralysing lethargy. As it was during a vacation, the usual props of study and university friends were withdrawn, and my mother was unavailable as ever, impatient or actively hostile to my moods (which were presumably threatening or incomprehensible to her). The trigger for my attempt was an incident in which she snapped at the sight of me in tears: 'You shouldn't think so much' – shorthand for 'feel so much'.

I don't think I can adequately describe the sense of utter rejection and loneliness this gave me, the vista of a closed circle in which my emotions were overpowering me (as if I were being attacked from within), and yet I was commanded to ignore them – a psychic impossibility.

On the evening of this day I returned from a futile meeting with the boyfriend who had left me, and banged my head repeatedly against the house wall, as if that could rid me of the unendurable pain I felt, or at least replace it with a bearable physical pain. All the clichés that used to evoke extraordinary states now took on a living force: I was literally out of my mind, beside myself with grief, and beneath this a complex, impotent anger and sense of betrayal at my parents' abandonment at crucial times over many years. I did not recognise this anger at the time, nor in a sense was I able to experience it properly (live it), even as it was crippling me. With hindsight, I can say that I needed to access the sources of all these powerful, flowing emotions and engage with them, but I had to have a guide, a support to do so.

The day after what felt like a final rejection, I was so frightened by my state that I begged my younger sister, who was still attending school, to come home early if possible, because I was terrified of being alone. When both she and my parents had gone, I was left alone in the house and was overwhelmed with anguish again. At this stage I was still fighting an impulse not simply to kill myself, but to 'destroy' myself – to be rid of all feeling. This stage of living, active struggle was succeeded by a terrible passivity and near calm. I ceased to hope or battle; I felt a complete inevitability. It was as if I were entering the acute stage of an illness, the culmination of the strange alternating state I had been in for weeks: intense painful feeling alternating with a hopelessness and extreme lethargy.

Once I had given in I felt a certain relief. I wanted oblivion and imagined death would be peaceful – a permanent sleep. When I actually began to take the aspirins, it was more difficult than I expected. I had to force them down and that was lonely and frightening. Even at this stage, at some level I think I wanted to be interrupted, found. The calm followed again. I curled up on the floor and waited to lose consciousness. After several hours I was still awake. I began to feel very ill and afraid, and it was as if another, rational part of me now took over. I rang the sister I was closest to and told her what I had done. She took immediate control, ringing an ambulance and rushing home to be with me. I was taken to a hospital where my stomach was pumped. I spent a strange hallucinatory night, unable to sleep, with my ears ringing with tinnitus from the aspirins. I passed in and out of waking dreams between bouts of sickness.

What I remember most of that night is the practical kindness of the black nurse on night duty who must have been cursing an extra 'self-inflicted' patient. She said very little to me, but her manner was humane. I fell asleep sometime in the early morning and woke later to find three young doctors looking down at me. They asked me a few questions, which I could not really answer, but seemed, above all, bemused. Later a woman hospital psychiatrist came to see me, and she effectively fed me a superficial diagnosis along the lines of 'It was a silly accident, wasn't it?' to which I weakly agreed, from awkwardness, confusion and exhaustion, probably also to distance myself. The whole experience, and perhaps its physicality, had provided a temporary exorcism. Underneath, my feelings remained.

Shortly after this very brief conversation I was discharged home. Both my parents and I were bewildered and wary with each other, but this time my mother took action and arranged for me to see a psychoanalyst recommended to her by a colleague. My meeting with him marked the first time anyone tried seriously to understand what I had been going through. My feelings resurfaced frighteningly during our meeting, but a lifeline had been created, even though he was not able to take me on as a patient, since I wanted (or this may have simply been assumed by my parents – I don't remember) to return to university.

My analyst suggested I seek counselling at university while I continued my course, but I felt unable and unwilling to do this for a variety of reasons: I felt as if I were being sent away again by the one person who had shown understanding, and also I had a superstitious feeling that I should be unable to complete my course if I were also undergoing counselling (I think I was partly right because it involves such a powerful journey and I wasn't strong enough at that point). And the family embargo on emotional revelation remained internalised. I finally returned to my analyst some years later and began this delayed journey.

I worry writing this, that my suicide attempt – for all the rational filter that analysts and 12 years' distance have given it – will still seem incomprehensible to outsiders. My experience of those years is both remote and still raw to myself. Approaching even its edge has been overwhelming. At times I have to stop writing. Also, the more I try to explain, the more I have a strange and horrible feeling that I will not be understood. This goes deep and is related to my parents' rebuttals and refusals.

I don't know that I can finish the account well. By 'well' I mean clearly, so that the complex truth of what happened is conveyed. But, even as a professional writer, I find it impossible. I am so frightened of somehow tidying, smoothing things over, falsifying, but most of all I am frightened of being misunderstood – still – of this account being 'rejected', going unheard, being discounted or disconfirmed. Because those were all the things which happened to me as a child and teenager within the family, which were reactivated by any external rejection and which ended in my suicide attempt. Although it is truer to speak of it as my 'suicide', as I began to realise later, because it was a kind of death and then, very slowly, over years of psychoanalysis, a kind of rebirth.

It has taken many years to understand what I have tried to convey of the feelings which led to suicide, both within a long, careful process of psychoanalysis and afterwards. I am still absolutely certain that without the most skilled, patient professional help I might not have survived or, at best, would have lurched from intermittent crisis to crisis. This help was not available at the hospital where I was taken and this is one reason I wanted to write my account, so that others will fare better than I initially did. I was privileged to see an excellent, empathic analyst, and particularly lucky because the 'match' was somehow right for me – or at least I was made to feel it was, simply by being met at the centre of my hurt.

The process (of analysis) I underwent was both basic and profound; basic in that I developed a primary and secure sense of self that I lacked before. (I think of it as the pieces knitting together to form a solid core – I'm far from immune to emotional storms, whether others' or my own, but now I can weather them.) The analysis was profound in that the process still informs my life today. I not only understand some of the forces which shaped me, but have a much greater understanding or intuition of those which shaped my parents' and even my grandparents' lives. I continue to explore these, and events have come to light which have enlarged my understanding further.

One of my sisters also embarked on psychotherapy later, perhaps in part because my experience had paved the way a little. And I think my analysis had a subtle effect on the whole family.

Perhaps, most importantly, I am now a mother myself, something I could never have dreamt, conceived, prior to my analysis, and that has been immensely reparative.

I think now that my suicide, which might only have been destructive – to others as well as myself – became instead creative of a new life. My journey continues and I hope that others can be helped by having the right kind of intervention early enough, but that depends on many things: primarily a much greater education about mental health issues, the creation of new specialist services, and effective publicity, particularly for young people.

Chapter 12

Conclusion

What have our suicidal patients taught us about the pre-suicide state of mind? First, we learned about the importance of listening to the patient, to their histories. The pre-suicide state of mind has a history. If we ignored our suicidal patients' histories or colluded with them in ignoring their history, our patients were likely to move from telling us about themselves to showing us by enacting a suicide fantasy.

Second, we learned to listen to the nature of their relationships and to what was going on in their lives before they tried to kill themselves. We learned that suicide is not a solipsistic, solitary act but always exists in the context of a primary relationship, which the patient depends upon for their psychic survival. We learned that a pre-suicide state of mind develops in response to the failure of the primary relationships.

Third, we learned to listen and pay heed to the patient's unconscious. This meant not only listening to what the patient says but also to what the patient does not say, or minimises, or denies. We learned that the motivating forces of a suicidal act reside in the unconscious. Their origins are found in the conscious and unconscious wishes of the parents and the experiences of the child from conception onwards, through infancy and childhood, to adolescence and adulthood. Suicide both reflects childhood conflicts and aims to reverse them, but at the cost of life itself.

Fourth, we learned from our pre-suicidal patients just how painful psychoanalytic psychotherapy or psychoanalysis is for them and for the therapist. For this reason we learned to listen to our own unconscious, our countertransference and affective reactions in order to recognise our own resistance, denial and avoidance of the pain, suffering and danger inherent in our patient's pre-suicidal state of mind. It was tempting at times for both patient and analyst to give up. But it is crucial not to abandon the therapeutic process despite the pressures to do so. The word crisis has come to connote a situation with potential for danger; but the original meaning is broader – it is a turning point, a crossroads, a state of affairs in which a decisive change for better or for worse is imminent.

The pre-suicide state of mind is a mind in crisis that is balanced between acting out a destructive fantasy or learning from the fantasy. Suicide may always remain an option for some suicidal individuals, but it is our belief that some resolution of the underlying conflicts will play a crucial part in reducing the suicidal potential.

Index

A&E (accident & emergency
    departments) 2, 27, 36, 81, 88
abandonment 34–5, 86, 107
Abelin, E. 58
abuse 15, 102–3
account, patient 105–10
acting out 24–6, 76
Adams, K. S. 21–2
addictions 13, 38, 51–3
Adler, Alfred 18
adolescence: assassination fantasies
    46–7; body image, and impact of
    puberty 65–8; development, and
    puberty 63–65; experimentation in
    65; female body image 66–7,
    71–2; group therapy 88;
    homosexuality in 68–70; male
    body image 67–8, 71;
    masturbation 71–2; pre-genital
    needs 45–6; pre-suicide state in
    63–72; risk in 65; self-mutilation
    99; sexual risks 85; suicide figures
    63
affective disorder 15, 16
affective responses 54, 99
aggression 14–15, 18, 31–3, 81
aggressor, identification with 60, 67,
    70–1, 85
Akhtar, S. 21, 65
alcohol abuse 15
alcoholism 13, 38
Allolio, B. 101
altruism 70–1
Alvarez, A. 80
Amos, T. 12

anal phase 100
analysis, process of 109–10
Anderson, Robin 7
Andreasen, N. 13
anomic suicide 9
anorexia nervosa 65, 67
antidepressants 3, 12, 53
anxiety disorders 15, 84–5
'anxious clinging' attachment 23
appetite disturbance 13
Appleby, L 12
Apter, A. 14–15, 23
Aragonès, E. 12
argumentativeness 13
Åsberg, M. 40
asceticism, definition 70
Asch, S. S. 27, 48, 54–5, 74, 76
aspirin, use of 9, 106
assassination fantasies 46–7, 77–8
assessments 13, 14, 16–17, 30, 80–4
assumptions 8, 9, 94
attachment 21–3, 58, 68, 83
attitudes, towards suicide 7–10

Barnett, B. 41
Baumert, J. 83–5
behavioural therapies 12
Bell, D. 21, 40
Bentley, H. 63
bereavement, suicide 40–1
Berrios, G. E. 8
betrayal 34–5
bi-sexuality 66
Bientema, H. 92
bipolar disorder 15, 16

Biven, B. 65, 99
blackmail 44, 53, 55, 76–7, 80
body barrier 38–41, 84
body image, and impact of puberty
    65–8
bondage 45
borderline personality disorder 13, 15
Bowlby, John 21
Braithwaite, R. 12
Briggs, S. 89
Brownscombe Heller, M. 88
Buie, D. H. 27, 46, 49
Buongiorno, P. A. 92

Campbell, D. 36, 43, 49, 51–3, 62
case studies: An assassination 47;
    Daughter and mother 36–7; 'Get a
    life' 37; Learning from a suicide
    attempt 105–10; An opportunity
    lost 85; An opportunity not lost
    85–6; The reckless driver 47–8; A
    revenge fantasy 44; Self-
    punishment fantasy and
    eroticization in a completed
    suicide 45; The stomach washout
    81; Taking responsibility for a
    body … 88; The uncle and the
    rock 79 See also 'Mr Adams'
    (case study)
casualty departments 2, 27, 36, 81, 88
Chasseguet-Smirgal, J. 66
childbirth 16
childhood: abuse 15, 102; daughter
    and mother (case study) 36–7;
    experiences 31–2; fantasies 43;
    lack of emotion in 106; 'organised
    insecure attachment' 23; trauma
    15, 21–2, 24–5, 37, 47–8; use of
    defences in 20
children: and anal phase 100; and
    mother 98–9, 102; relationship
    with parents 19–20, 36–7, 47–8,
    51–3, 64; suicide figures 63;
    unconscious processes 19–20
Chin, A. 15–16
cognitive behavioural therapy (CBT)
    12
Coid, J. 101
confusion 38–9, 66, 99

conscious processes 8, 22, 38, 43
'constriction' (pre-suicidal) 35
contemporary psychoanalytic
    understanding 21–4
control, in relationships 33, 35
coping mechanisms 14–15
Core Complex 24, 30–41, 47, 99
coroner's court 94–5
countertransference 24, 54–5, 80, 89,
    99
Crawford, M. J. 27
Crouch, W. 89
Cunningham, C. 15–16
current life situation, danger signals
    76–9

Daldin, H. 65
danger signals: current life situation
    76–9; historical 13–14, 75–6;
    Rorschach test 40; within the
    transference 79–80
deception 79, 94
defences, using 14–15, 20, 70, 82, 88
Delirium Tremens 38
delusions 26, 47, 60, 65, 78, 103
denial 82–3, 84, 88, 91
Department of Health (UK) 16, 63,
    82
dependence 84
depression 12, 13, 15, 16, 23, 105
Devices of Suicide 27, 46, 48, 49
diagnostic assessments 16–17
dialectical behavioural therapy (DBT)
    12
dicing-with-death fantasy 45, 47–8,
    53, 74
displacement 15, 101
dissociation 15
drug dependency 13
Durkheim, E. 8, 18
dyadic relationship, failure of 40
dynamic constriction, definition 35–6

eating disorders 65, 67
Edman, G. 40
ego 19, 20–1, 23, 38, 39
elderly people 15–16
'encaptive' conflict 99
endorphin levels 101

Erazo, N. 83–5
Essential Papers on Suicide
  (Maltsberger and Goldblatt) 8
excitability 13
excretory functions 100
executioner, analyst as 48, 55, 74, 86
experimentation 65
Exploring in Security: ... (Holmes)
  23
external action 75
external factors 18, 102
external objects 39

Fagg, J. 75
failure 14, 40, 76, 82, 105
families, effect on 110
family member, suicide/attempt by
  59–60, 75–6, 79
family therapy 84
fantasies: assassination 46–7, 77–8;
  case studies 44, 59–62; consent/
  collusion between patient and
  others 77–8; of death 20, 108;
  dicing-with-death 45, 47–8, 53,
  74; escape route 105; feared 86;
  masturbation 71; merging 48;
  murderous 87; Oedipal 64, 68,
  101; between patient and others
  84; and pre-suicide state 43–9;
  psychoanalytic understanding of
  26–8; revenge 22, 44; self-
  punishment 44–6; sexual 70;
  unconscious and 8, 25–6, 45
father: and daughter 58, 59, 66–7,
  102; role of the 57–62; and son
  51–3, 57, 58–60, 67, 69, 77–8
Federn, P. 70
female body image, in adolescence
  66–7, 71–2
femininity 58, 67, 69, 102
fetishism 20, 45
Fitch, K. 63
Foley, S. 89
Forsti, H. 83–5
Freud, Anna 70
Freud, Sigmund: acting out 24–5;
  'the exception' 47; father-
  daughter relationship 58;
  homosexuality 69; 'Mourning and

Melancholia' 5, 18–21; 'The
  Transformations of Puberty' 65–6
Friedlander, K. 48
Friedman, Maurice 5

gambling 51–3
Gardner, F. 99
Geddes, J. 13
Gelder, M 13
genitalia 65, 67, 71, 101–2
Gitlin, M. J. 92
Glasser, Mervin 30, 31, 69
Goldblatt, M. J. 8
Goldstein, L. S. 92
Gosliner, B. J. 58
GPs, visits to 12–13
Greenson, R. 58
Gutheil, Emil 79

Haas, A. P. 90
Hale, R. 27, 41, 43, 49, 56, 85–6
hallucinations 14
Harker, L. 63
Hawton, K. 8, 75
Henderson, S. 21
Hendin, H. 90
Hendrick, I 48
historical: danger signals 13–14,
  75–6; psychoanalytic
  understanding 18–21
Holmes, Jeremy 5, 23
homicide 39, 59
homosexuality, in adolescence
  68–70
hospital staff, unsympathetic 81
Housman, A. E. 1, 38
humiliation 14, 19, 34–5
husband-wife relationship 57–8

identification: with aggressor 60, 67,
  70–1, 85; of the ego 19; with
  parents 39, 48, 57–60, 102;
  projective 25, 27, 31 *See also*
  body image, and impact of
  puberty
illegality, of suicide 8
illusion 26, 92
implications, for the professional
  74–95

imprisonment 8, 103
impulsion 14–15
incest 66
inquest, coroner's 94–5
instinct 5, 19, 20, 21, 24, 46
institutions, psychiatric 87, 93–4,
    103
intellectualisation 70–1, 91
internal conflicts 22–3, 31, 75
intervention, professional 72, 84, 92,
    106–7, 110
intrusion 99

Jenkins, G. R. 27
Joseph, B. 97
'jumper' (train) 55
Jutte, S. 63

Kamerow, D. 11
Kelly, B. 89
Kettlewell, Caroline 100, 101
Kind, Jurgen 23–4
King, Pearl 52, 54, 99
Klein, M. 27
Kleinian perspective 40, 64
Krawitz, M. 83–5

Labad, A. 12
Ladwig, K. H. 83–5
Laufer, Egle 5, 46, 55, 66, 67, 71
Laufer, Moses 5, 46, 55, 66, 67, 71
Lawlor, B. A. 15–16
Lemma, Alessandra 89, 103
libido 20
Lipschitz, A. 90
listening, as professionals 27, 51–5,
    111
Litman, R.E. 19–20, 45
Loewald, H. W. 58
loneliness 11, 53, 106, 107
Lonnquist, J. K. 13
Lopez-Ibor, J. 13
Lukaschek, K. 83–5
Luoma, J. B. 12

McCarthy, C. 97, 101, 102
Mahler, M. S. 58
male body image, in adolescence
    67–8, 71

Maltsberger, J. T. 8, 27, 39, 46, 49,
    90
management, of a suicide attempt
    80–8
manic-depression 13, 15
Martin, C. E. 12
masturbation 44–6, 45, 70, 71–2
medication 16, 53
melancholia 18–19, 20–1
men 11, 51–3, 63
mental illnesses 11–17, 12, 14, 15
merging fantasies 48
middle-aged men 11
Miller, P. 63
mother: and children 98–9, 102; and
    daughter 36–7, 66, 67, 106, 107,
    108; rejection by 21, 30–2, 47–8,
    106–7; and son 51–3, 58–62, 68,
    77–8
Motz, A. 100
'Mourning and Melancholia' (Freud)
    18–19
'Mr Adams' (case study) 51–3,
    59–62, 75–9, 80
Mulder, T. 92
multidimensional approach 12
'mummy's boy' 51–3
Murphy, T. 63

narcissism 14, 20, 51, 79, 99
National Society for Prevention of
    Cruelty to Children (report) 63
neuroticism 23, 65
NICE (National Institute for Health
    and Care Excellence) 82

'object,' the body as an 27–8, 30
O'Connell, H. 15–16
Oedipal: complex 64–5; needs 51, 64,
    66–8, 72, 101, 103; negative
    phase 69; positive phase 69; pre-
    46, 57–8, 59, 66–8
Office for National Statistics (UK)
    63
Ogden, T. H. 25
oral incorporative impulses 44, 45
oral phase 98–9, 101, 103
overdoses 9, 36, 81, 86, 106, 108
oversensitivity 14–15

painkillers 9, 53
Papanastassiou, M. 27
paranoia 40, 47, 65
parents, and children: daughter
    and mother (case study) 36–7;
    'Get a life' (case study) 37; Mr
    Adams (case study) 51–3; patient
    account 106; reckless driver (case
    study) 47–8; relationship with
    19–20, 64, 108; revenge fantasy
    (case study) 44 See also father;
    mother
patient account 105–10
Pearson, J. L. 12
perceptions, distortion of 14, 26
Perelberg, R. J. 44
perfectionism 14
'perpetrator' 22, 32, 40–1, 71
personal reactions, to suicide of a
    patient 90–3
personality constellations 14–17
personality disorders 13, 15
pharmacological treatment 3, 12, 14
physical abuse 15, 102
Piñol, J. L. 12
plans, suicide 78–9
Pollet, S. 88
Pollock, G. H. 41
Porter, R. 8
post mortem, psychiatric 92–3
post mortem, psychological 88–9
post-partum suicide 16
post-traumatic stress disorder 55, 91,
    95
pre-genital: anxiety 68; needs 44, 46,
    71
pre-suicide state: in adolescence
    63–72; and Erwin Ringel 35–6;
    role of the father 57–62; and
    suicide fantasies 43–9
prevention strategies 11
professional: care 12, 16; impact of
    suicide on 89–90; implications for
    the 74–95; intervention 72, 84, 92,
    106–7, 110; listening 27, 51–5,
    111; reaction to patient's suicide
    89–90
projection 25, 30, 31, 49, 65, 70
promiscuity 85

psychiatric: diagnoses 13; institutions
    87, 93–4, 103; post mortem 92–3;
    secondary services 12–13
psychiatrists, view of suicide 11
psychiatry, organic 12
psychoanalysis: acting out 24–6;
    approach 16; contemporary 21–4;
    fantasies 26–8; historically 18–21;
    process 8; treatment 9
psychoanalysts 8, 12, 21
psychological autopsy, definition 12
psychological post mortem 88–9
psychologists, view of suicide 12
psychopathic disorders 13
psychotherapists 12
psychotic illnesses 13–14, 15, 23, 40,
    47
puberty, and adolescent development
    63–65

quasi-delusional, suicide as 22

rationalisation 9, 91
Rees, L. H. 101
regression 14–15, 30, 33, 48, 55,
    98–100
rejection: fear of 86; minor 33; by
    mother 21, 30–2, 47–8, 106–7;
    physical gestures 37; self-
    mutilation 99; verbal 37, 77
relationships: controlling 33, 35;
    difficulty forming 22; failure of
    76, 82, 105, 106
relatives, suicide/attempt by 59–60,
    75–6, 79
reliability, of therapist 83–4, 87
religion, and suicide 8
'repetition compulsion' (Freud) 25
repression 9, 35, 43, 64, 82, 84
revenge suicide fantasies 22, 44
reverse transference 52
Richman, J. 84
Ringel, Erwin 35, 36, 43
risk: in adolescence 65, 85; -aversive
    culture 87; factors 11, 14–15;
    taking 47–8
Rorschach test 39–40
Rosenbaum, M. 84
Rydin, E. 40

sadism 18, 32, 40, 41
sadomasochism 32–3, 35, 44–6, 55,
    77, 82
Sandler, J. 54
Savage God, The (Alvarez) 80
Schachter, Joan 30
Schalling, D. 40
schizoid personality disorder (SPD)
    14, 23
schizophrenia 13–14, 15, 40, 47
secrecy 78, 94
self-defence, suicide as 47
self-harm, definition 97
self-mutilation 10, 47, 51, 67, 88,
    97–103
self-mutilation, definition 98
self-punishment, suicide as 19,
    44–6
self-purification 101–2
self-wounding, definition 97–8
Serious Incident Inquiry (Serious
    Untoward Incident – SUI) 93–4
serotonin metabolism, disturbance of
    15
sexual abuse 102–3
sexual energy 20
sexual reassignment surgery (SRS)
    103
Shakespeare, William 7
shame 14, 66, 90
Shaw, J. 12
Shooter, Mike 88
sibling support 106, 107, 108
signals, danger: current life situation
    76–9; historical 13–14, 75–6;
    Rorschach test 39–40; within the
    transference 79–80
Singapore, and attempted suicide 8
situational constriction, definition 35
skin, as a medium 99–100
Skin Game (Kettlewell) 100
sleep disturbance 13
sociologists, view of suicide 11
splitting, of the ego 21, 23–4, 30, 46,
    48, 60
statistics 11, 12–13, 63
Stekel, Wilhelm 18, 64, 90
Stern, D. N. 27, 30
stomach washouts 81, 108

Straker, M. 54, 77
substance abuse 15
suicidal act, definition 10
suicidal process 33–4
suicide, aftermath of 88–9
suicide attempt: body barrier 38–41;
    case study 105–10; confusion
    38–9; the trigger 37–8
suicide fantasies 22, 26–8, 43–9, 77,
    78 *See also* 'Mr Adams' (case
    study)
suicide figures: adolescence 63;
    depressive orders and 12; in UK
    11, 63; in US 12–13, 63
suicide index 40
superego 20–1, 38, 71, 79
Swearingen, C. 19, 45

Tahka, V. A. 55, 79
Talion, principle of 2, 64
theoretical frameworks 11–12
transference: counter- 24, 54–5, 80,
    89, 99; and danger signals 79–80;
    to a father 61–2; reverse 52
'The Transformations of Puberty'
    (Freud) 65–6
transitional domains 23–4
trigger, the 37–8
Troquete, N. 92
Tyler, Andrew 55
Tyrer, P. 27

UK Government Confidential Inquiry
    (1997) 12
unconscious processes: anger 15;
    children and 19–20; concept of 8;
    confusion 38; countertransference
    54; and fantasies 45; identification
    60; scrutiny of 9, 22; sleep 48
unipolar affective disorder 16
unpredictability, in adolescence 65
US, suicide figures 12–13, 63

Valium 51, 53, 60, 78
Van den Brink, R. 92
van Heeringen, K. 8
'victim' 40–1
Vienna Psychoanalytic Society
    symposium 18, 64

violence 16, 31–3, 37–8, 40

*Webster's New International
   Dictionary* 26
wife-husband relationship 57–8
Wohl, Myer 5
women 63, 103

World Health Organisation (WHO)
   11
wounds 85, 88, 97–8, 100, 102
Wynecoop, S. 90

Zilborg, G. 44

 Taylor & Francis eBooks

Helping you to choose the right eBooks for your Library

Add Routledge titles to your library's digital collection today. Taylor and Francis ebooks contains over 50,000 titles in the Humanities, Social Sciences, Behavioural Sciences, Built Environment and Law.

Choose from a range of subject packages or create your own!

Benefits for you

» Free MARC records
» COUNTER-compliant usage statistics
» Flexible purchase and pricing options
» All titles DRM-free.

Benefits for your user

» Off-site, anytime access via Athens or referring URL
» Print or copy pages or chapters
» Full content search
» Bookmark, highlight and annotate text
» Access to thousands of pages of quality research at the click of a button.

 REQUEST YOUR **FREE** INSTITUTIONAL TRIAL TODAY

Free Trials Available
We offer free trials to qualifying academic, corporate and government customers.

eCollections – Choose from over 30 subject eCollections, including:

Archaeology	Language Learning
Architecture	Law
Asian Studies	Literature
Business & Management	Media & Communication
Classical Studies	Middle East Studies
Construction	Music
Creative & Media Arts	Philosophy
Criminology & Criminal Justice	Planning
Economics	Politics
Education	Psychology & Mental Health
Energy	Religion
Engineering	Security
English Language & Linguistics	Social Work
Environment & Sustainability	Sociology
Geography	Sport
Health Studies	Theatre & Performance
History	Tourism, Hospitality & Events

For more information, pricing enquiries or to order a free trial, please contact your local sales team: www.tandfebooks.com/page/sales

 Routledge Taylor & Francis Group | The home of Routledge books

www.tandfebooks.com